D1711379

Education and Career Choice

Also by Patrick White

TEACHER SUPPLY: The Issues (*With S. Gorard, E. Smith and B. H. See*)

Education and Career Choice

A New Model of Decision Making

Patrick White
University of Leicester, UK

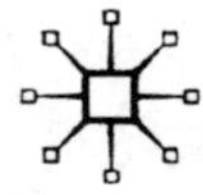

First published in 2007 by
PALGRAVE MACMILLAN
Houndmills, Basingstoke, Hampshire RG21 6XS and
175 Fifth Avenue, New York, N.Y. 10010
Companies and representatives throughout the world.

PALGRAVE MACMILLAN is the global academic imprint of the Palgrave Macmillan division of St. Martin's Press, LLC and of Palgrave Macmillan Ltd. Macmillan® is a registered trademark in the United States, United Kingdom and other countries. Palgrave is a registered trademark in the European Union and other countries.

ISBN-13: 978–1–4039–8623–8 hardback
ISBN-10: 1–4039–8623–1 hardback

This book is printed on paper suitable for recycling and made from fully managed and sustained forest sources.

A catalogue record for this book is available from the British Library.

Library of Congress Cataloging-in-Publication Data

White, Patrick, 1971–
Education and career choice : a new model of decision making / Patrick White.
p. cm.
Includes bibliographical references and index.
Contents: Education and career decision making : an introduction to the issues – Methods, context and sample – Contextualising post-sixteen transitions : national, regional and historical trends – Conceptualising choice : types, stages and models – Choice motivations in year 9 – Choice factors and rationales in year 11 – Destinations, aspirations and trajectories – Concluding remarks.
ISBN-13: 978–1–4039–8623–8 (cloth)
ISBN-10: 1–4039–8623–1 (cloth)
1. Student aspirations – Great Britain. 2. Vocational interests – Great Britain. 3. High school graduates – Great Britain – Attitudes. I. Title.

LA637.7.W45 2007
373.1'80941—dc22 2006050005

10 9 8 7 6 5 4 3 2 1
16 15 14 13 12 11 10 09 08 07

Printed and bound in Great Britain by
Antony Rowe Ltd, Chippenham and Eastbourne

Contents

List of Tables vi

List of Figures viii

Abbreviations and Terms x

Acknowledgements xii

Introduction xiii

1 Educational and Career Decision Making: An Introduction to the Issues 1

2 Methods, Context and Sample 35

3 Contextualising Post-16 Transitions: National, Regional and Historical Trends 47

4 Conceptualising Choice: Types, Stages and Models 83

5 Choice Motivations in Year 9 106

6 Choice Factors and Rationales in Year 11 122

7 Destinations, Aspirations and Trajectories 153

8 Concluding Remarks 167

Appendix 172

Bibliography 179

Index 187

List of Tables

3.1 All learners in further education, by sex, United Kingdom, 1970/71–2001/02 54
3.2 All learners in further education, by mode of study, United Kingdom, 1970/71–2001/02 55
3.3 Learners on Council-funded FE provision, by age and qualification aim level, England, 2004/05 56
3.4 Higher Education participation rates by social class groups 1990 and 2000 59
3.5 Pupils aged 15 achieving GCSE/GNVQ grades by school type, England, 2003/04 64
3.6 Average GCE/VCE A/AS-level point score of 16–18 year-old candidates by type of institution and gender, England, 2004/05 70
3.7 Main study aim of 16 year-olds: by parents' qualifications, England and Wales, 2000 71
3.8 Average point score of 16–18 year-old candidates entered for GCE/VCE A/AS-levels, by Government Office Region, 2004/05 72
5.1 Year 9 choice motivations – by frequency 118
6.1 Choice factors and choice stages 146
6.2 The relationship between factors and rationales: all students 147
7.1 Post-16 intentions and occupational aspirations by gender and occupational class 157
7.2 Occupational aspirations and social mobility 158
A1 Indices of income and employment, by Local Authority, 2004 173
A2 Income-based job seekers allowance claimants as percentage of population, August 2003 173
A3 Qualification levels of resident population aged 16–74, April 2001 174

A4 Distribution of ethnic groups, by Local Authority and Region, 2001 175
A5 Characteristics of schools in the sample, 1997/98 176
A6 Composition of sample by occupational class and sex 178

List of Figures

3.1	Young people aged 16–18 years in education and training by sex, England, 1986 to 1999	49
3.2	Participation in post-16 education and training, by route, England, 1994–2003	50
3.3	Male participation in post-16 education and training, England, 1986–1999	51
3.4	Female participation in post-16 education and training, England 1986–1999	52
3.5	Age participation index, Great Britain, 1990/91–2001/02	57
3.6	Age participation index by social class, Great Britain, 1990–2001	58
3.7	Higher Education participation rates by social class groups, 1960–2000	58
3.8	Pupils aged 15 achieving 5+ GCSEs/GNVQs at grades A* to C, England, 1988/89–2003/04	61
3.9	Pupils aged 15 with no GCSE/GNVQ passes, England, 1988/89–2003/04	62
3.10	Achievement at GCE A-level or equivalent, United Kingdom, 1992/93–2001/02	66
3.11	Percentage of 16–18 year-old candidates achieving two or more GCE/VCE A-level passes in schools and FE colleges, in England, 1993/94–2004/05	67
3.12	General Certificate of Secondary Education A-level pass rate (%), by sex, 1995/96–2004/05	68
3.13	Distribution of GCSE A-level grades, as percentage passes, 1995/96–2004/05	69
3.14	General Certificate of Secondary Education A-level entries, growing subject areas, 1995/96–2004/05	75
3.15	General Certificate of Secondary Education A-level entries, subject areas in decline, 1995/96–2004/05	76

3.16 General Certificate of Education A-level or equivalent entries for young people, selected subjects, United Kingdom, 2001/02 77
3.17 Distribution of GCE A-level grades, selected subjects, England, 2003/04 78
4.1 Choice in Year 9 (GCSE options) – version 1 99
4.2 Choices in Year – version 2 100
4.3 Year 11 choice model – version 1 101
4.4 Year 11 choice model – version 2 102
4.5 Year 9 choice frequencies 103
4.6 Year 11 choice, by 'type' and 'stage' 104
A1 Pupils achieving five or more GCSE A*–C grades, Lumbertonshire LEA and England, 1996–2004 174
A2 Pupils achieving five or more GCSEs at A*–C, by school, 1994–2004 177

Abbreviations and Terms

API	Age participation index (higher education)
AVCE	Advanced vocational certificate in education
BTEC	Business and Technology Education Council
CEG	Careers education and guidance
DfEE	Department for Education and Employment (now DfES)
DfES	Department for Education and Skills
DOVE	Diploma of Vocational Education
ESRC	Economic and Social Research Council
FE	Further Education
GCE A-level	General Certificate of Education, Advanced level
GCE AS-level	General Certificate of Education, Advanced subsidiary level
GCSE	General Certificate of Secondary Education
GNVQ	General National Vocational Qualification
HE	Higher education
HEFC	Higher Education Funding Council
HESA	Higher Education Statistics Agency
IER	Initial entry rate
LA	Local authority
LEA	Local education authority
LFS	Labour Force Survey
LSC	Learning and Skills Council
NCDS	National Child Development Study
NVQ	National Vocational Qualification
ONS	Office for National Statistics
SES	Socio-economic status
SSLS	Scottish School Leavers Survey
UCAS	University and Colleges Admissions Service
VCE A-level	Vocational Certificate of Education, Advanced level

VCE AS-level	Vocational Certificate of Education, Advanced subsidiary level
YCS	Youth Cohort Study
. . .	Pause in interview conversation
[. . .]	Section of interview conversation edited for presentation

Acknowledgements

I would first like to thank all the students and staff who participated in the fieldwork and without whom the research project could not have been conducted. I would also like to thank the following people for their help, advice and guidance during the research and the writing of this book. Thank you to Jane Salisbury and Gareth Rees, for much encouragement and support during my research. Thanks also to John Fitz for reading my work early in the research. I am grateful to Stephen Gorard for a thorough reading of this text and for inspiration and encouragement over the past few years. Thank you to Emma Smith for her endless patience and support in the face of much impatience and frustration. She also provided valuable advice to a new author. I would finally like to thank my parents, Beryl and Michael, for all their support over the years. This book is dedicated to them.

Introduction

This is a book about choice. Choice is an emotive subject among social scientists as it is of central importance to debates in a wide range of substantive areas. The relative importance of individual freedom of action ('agency') and the constraints imposed by one's position in society ('structure') has been fiercely debated and there are few, if any, areas of study within the social sciences where questions relating to individual choice are not raised. Consequently, the literature in the area is wide ranging both in terms of disciplinary origin and topic of investigation.

The research documented in this text is, in the context of the above, very modest in both its scope and ambitions. Its primary goal was to attempt to examine decision-making behaviour in a particular context, the transition facing young people nearing the end of their compulsory schooling in the United Kingdom. Payne (2003, p. 8) highlights the importance of this area of study stating that

> the choices that young people make about what to do at age 16 when compulsory full-time education ends are of both private and public interest. Their choices affect both their own futures and the supply of educated and trained labour in the economy.

There were two main elements to the research project. A review and synthesis of the available secondary data identified important trends in post-16 participation. The fieldwork, primarily involving interviews with young people, aimed to conceptualise the choice-making process at this important transition.

As the fieldwork was conducted over a certain period of time and in a specific geographical location, any findings are limited by this. Any attempts to generalise the findings generated by analysis of the interview data must, necessarily, be speculative. However, the study described herein represents an attempt to move the field forward in several different ways.

First, in contrast to other studies examining choice at this juncture, the analysis attempts to present a model that represents, however approximately, the *process* of decision making. While previous studies of post-16 choice have purported to investigate the process of choice (e.g. Hodkinson *et al.* 1996) any resulting models have been inadequate, for reasons that are explained in Chapter 1. Secondly, the concepts used in the present study to describe the choice process do not rely on either problematic or contested notions, such as rationality, or the work of currently fashionable theorists. Finally, while not attempting to replicate the large-scale surveys documenting the factors influencing young people's decisions, the study incorporates students' motivations and ambitions into the analyses.

Unlike most small-scale studies, the sample of institutions and students in this study are located in local, regional and national contexts through an examination of secondary data relating to participation and attainment. Although this does not increase the generalisability of the findings, it 'sets the scene' for the study whilst allowing the reader to make judgements regarding the typicality of both the individuals and institutions that participated in the research.

Chapter 1 locates the present study in the context of wider debates surrounding both youth transitions, and educational and career choice. The theoretical frameworks that have previously been used to conceptualise youth transitions are examined, with particular attention paid to debates relating to the reproduction of inequalities. The role played by theory in recent empirical research is questioned, alongside an evaluation of the usefulness of currently fashionable, and frequently cited, theoretical concepts.

Previous research into post-16 transitions is reviewed in detail in order to assess the current state of knowledge in the area. Important predictors of both continued participation and particular routes are identified, as are factors and sources of information identified by young people as influential on their choices.

The chapter ends with a detailed examination of the work of two groups of researchers whose research has been particularly influential. Problems relating to these researchers' operationalisation of social class are highlighted, as is their reliance on problematic theoretical concepts. Their contribution to an understanding of the *process* of post-16 choice is also questioned.

Chapter 2 outlines the methods of data collection and analysis used in the research. The collection and analysis of secondary data is addressed first. The value of, and problems inherent to, an analysis of existing large scale data sets is discussed, and the sources used are described briefly. The fieldwork element of the research is then addressed, beginning with an account of the selection of both the institutional and student samples and their resulting composition. The limitations placed on the research by the methods of data collection and the nature of the sample are discussed, and their implications for any findings explored.

Chapter 3 uses publicly available data to map recent trends in post-16 participation and attainment. Pertinent data relating to compulsory schooling and higher education (HE) are also examined. Analyses of Department for Education and Skills (DfES) and Youth Cohort Study (YCS) data are used, alongside other relevant data sets, to map important trends and developments and to place the research within a national context. Important long term trends and changes occurring since the study took place are also documented and reflected upon.

Chapter 4 is the first of four chapters documenting the results of the analysis of the student interviews. It describes the first stages of the analysis of the interview data, which concentrated on the development of a typology of decision making. Decision making was conceptualised as being either 'inclusive', 'exclusive' or 'default'. This typology was combined with the idea of choice 'stages' to construct models of decision making in Years 9 and 11.

Chapter 5 examines the motivations young people reported for particular choices made in Year 9. Connections are made between the particular types of choice behaviour observed in this year and the restricted nature of the alternatives available to students. Young people's orientations to their educational and vocational careers are also examined.

In Chapter 6 the motivations for Year 11 choices are considered. Because of both the richer nature of the interview data relating to this transition and the increased complexity of the choices to be made, the analysis is more sophisticated. Motivations are examined in terms of two related dimensions – 'factors' and 'rationales'. The connections between students' prioritising of different 'factors' and the 'rationales' they provided for their decisions are of particular concern.

Chapter 7 examines the occupational aspirations of the student sample. Young people's career goals are compared to their class backgrounds in order to assess their 'imagined mobility'. The place of occupational intentions in relation to post-16 choices is investigated and the idea of 'cumulative trajectories' is proposed.

Chapter 8 summarises the most important research findings and draws tentative conclusions. The current state of research in the area is also addressed and recommendations are made for future areas of study. The implications for recent policy debates are also explored.

Appendix A includes contextual information relating to the local area in which the fieldwork was conducted. Information on the following areas is included: the local labour market, unemployment, income, uptake of benefits, and levels of education. These data are then compared to national and regional averages. The relative position of the locale in relation to these indicators is assessed, alongside potential implications for the research. Brief descriptions of the educational institutions in the sample are also included, alongside data on their intake and academic outputs.

Research questions

It is useful for the reader of any research report to be clear about the aims of the study. The research questions addressed in this research can be summarised as follows:

1. In terms of the post-16 transition, what have been the most important trends in educational attainment and participation over the past two decades?
2. How do young people make educational and career decisions at the end of compulsory schooling?
3. What factors are considered important by different young people?
4. What motivates young people to make particular choices about their post-16 destinations?
5. What is the cumulative effect of decisions made during compulsory schooling on young people's career trajectories?

1
Educational and Career Decision Making: An Introduction to the Issues

The aim of this chapter is to locate the present study within the existing research on educational and career choice. It starts by examining youth transitions in fairly general terms but, as the chapter progresses, the discussion becomes more tightly focused on issues directly relating to the transition from compulsory schooling at the end of the 1990s. Particular attention is paid to attempts to describe and conceptualise the choice process, and to the work of researchers who have been particularly influential in recent times. Research on educational choice at other points of transition is drawn on, where appropriate, in order both to make comparisons and to assess the relevance of any findings for post-16 decision making.

Youth transitions research in late twentieth-century Britain

During the last three decades of the twentieth century, youth transitions at the end of compulsory schooling changed dramatically. In the 1960s and 1970s, when the majority of young people left school to enter the labour market, the type of decisions to be made were very different from those faced by students in the 1990s, when over 70 per cent of those finishing compulsory education entered further education and/or training (Furlong and Cartmel 1997). As a consequence of such changes, research in the area also changed, and so did the relevance of particular lines of enquiry. Some fundamental questions are of a 'perennial' nature, however, and continue to be of interest to social scientists working in the area (Roberts 1995). The following discussion traces the history of social scientific interest in youth transitions, and identifies both the changes and continuities in theoretical approaches that have taken place during the latter decades of the twentieth century.

Changing theoretical perspectives

In the late 1990s, several commentators attempted to provide an overview of theoretical perspectives in the area of youth transitions (e.g. Evans and Furlong 1997; Roberts 1997a; Rudd 1997), each varying in their conclusions but remarkable for their focus on particular issues. Evans and Furlong (1997) identify several 'metaphors' of youth transition corresponding to particular periods in the latter half of the twentieth century. In the 1960s, when employment opportunities were plentiful, concerns were focused on filling societies' 'niches', a perspective the authors associate with developmental psychology and functionalist sociology, both of which were popular at that time, especially in the United States. The rising unemployment of the 1970s led to a more protracted transition from school to work for some, and these changes were accompanied by a vocabulary of career 'pathways'. Debate in the 1980s was primarily concerned with 'trajectories', the influences of social structure being viewed as determinants of the labour market careers of individuals and larger groups, while the 1990s saw the emergence of a concern with the 'navigation' of an increasingly complex array of opportunities and risks.

As can be seen, the ways in which transitions have been conceptualised has often been strongly influenced by wider trends in the social scientific disciplines during particular periods. Roberts (1997a) argues that during the latter half of the twentieth century it has often been the case that the development of theory has out-paced empirical evidence (but that there have also been times when the reverse has been true). Indeed, many of these theoretical shifts merely reflect differences in beliefs about the relative importance of structure and agency in determining the destinations of young people. However, no amount of theoretical debate can resolve what is essentially an empirical question. The following sections look at these theoretical developments in greater detail, and examine the issues they raise with regard to post-16 transitions.

Setting the parameters: 'developmental' and 'opportunity structure' theories of career progression

The late 1960s gave rise to a dispute that set the parameters of discussions of youth transitions for the next twenty years. The debate was initiated by Roberts's (1968, 1975, 1977) criticisms of the theories of Super (1957, 1968) and Ginzberg *et al.* (1951), which were grounded in the principles of psychology and concentrated on expanding the vocational horizons of young people to avoid 'premature closure of occupational [aspirations]' (Furlong 1992, p. 111). In a seminal article, Roberts (1977) argued that these theories overemphasised the role of individual choice, pointing to the overwhelming empirical evidence demonstrating that occupational futures are governed primarily by the opportunity structure. He concluded that 'neither school-leavers nor adults typically "choose" occupations in any meaningful sense: they simply take what is available' (p. 1).

The conclusions of this argument were not only that '[careers] guidance has a limited role to play' (p. 9) but that individual choice was also constrained in its impact on the occupational futures of young people. While 'developmental' theories had concentrated on individual agency, Roberts emphasised the ways in which 'opportunity structures limit the genuine careers that are available [and] restrict the scope for individual occupational choice' (p. 4).

Roberts's article sparked a lively debate within the careers education and guidance (CEG) journals that provoked vociferous defences of the role of CEG programmes in schools, which at that time were predominantly based on the developmentalist theories. Ginzberg *et al.*'s (1951) original study has since been described, even by fellow developmentalists, as unconvincing in its methodology (Super 1981). Roberts, however, has been criticised by Furlong (1992) for misrepresenting the 'developmental' position, who argues that both Ginzberg and Super incorporated the influence of structural constraints into their theories.

The importance of this debate, however, goes beyond interpretations of the subtleties (or otherwise) of the arguments put forward by each side. Instead it lies in the application of a wider debate to this specific area of study. Resolution of this debate hinges on the relative importance of structure and agency in determining an individual's behaviour and the resulting consequences. In this particular context

Rudd and Evans have summarised it as 'the issue of young people's degrees of *control* over their career destinies' (1998, pp. 39–40, original emphasis). They expand the question in terms of

> the relative contributions of *agency* (input from young people themselves on an individual basis) and *structure* (inputs from organisations at a national and local level, the effects of labour markets, and influences of broad social characteristics such as gender, social class and ethnicity) on the education-to-employment transition process.
>
> (Rudd and Evans 1998, p. 39, original emphasis)

All subsequent theoretical conceptualisations of youth transitions have addressed this fundamental issue, albeit sometimes using different vocabularies. Roberts continued to develop the idea of the 'career trajectory' during the 1980s and 1990s (see Bynner and Roberts 1991; Roberts 1997a), acknowledging that although 'the processes whereby young people enter the labour market have undergone their most thorough overhaul since the advent of compulsory schooling' (Roberts 1997b, p. 345) it was important not to underestimate what Rudd and Evans (1998, p. 40) later referred to as 'the importance of structures in young people's lives, including dimensions of social class, gender and ethnicity and the influence of economic factors such as labour markets and unemployment rates'. Gottfredson (1981) refined the 'developmental' approach, paying greater attention to structural factors in the framing of individuals' occupational preferences, although his theorising was grounded in what Osipow (1990, p. 123) described as a 'sparse . . . empirical base'.

The degree to which young people's choices are constrained by external factors is central to the study of post-16 transitions. Particular forms of structural constraint, such as social class and educational background, have often been viewed as key determinants of the limited social mobility of particular social groups. This topic is examined below, with particular attention being paid to theoretical perspectives that were popular at the beginning of the twenty-first century.

Explanations of social reproduction

Although most researchers and theorists allowed at least some scope for individual choice, the fact that young peoples' social backgrounds are generally powerful predictors of their labour market futures has led to an understandable concern with the social reproduction of inequality. Whilst in the United Kingdom, Roberts (1968, 1977) documented the continuing influence of structural factors in the shaping of career trajectories, on the continent another approach was being developed. Bourdieu and Passeron's (1997) study of the education system in France was to become very influential, particularly in terms of the concept of 'cultural capital' that they employed in their explanation of social reproduction.

The work of Pierre Bourdieu (1986, Bourdieu and Passeron 1977) is often referred to in accounts of the role played by education in social reproduction, particularly in relation to the 'choice' of different education and training options (e.g. Gewirtz *et al.* 1995; Hodkinson *et al.* 1996; Foskett and Hesketh 1997; Ball *et al.* 2000; Reay 2002; Brooks 2003; Reay and Lucey 2003). Bourdieu's theory is neatly explained by Sullivan (2002a, p. 144) as follows.

> Success in the education system is facilitated by the possession of cultural capital and of higher class habitus. Lower-class pupils do not in general possess these traits, so the failure of the majority of these pupils is inevitable. This explains class inequalities in educational attainment.

Despite the notoriously difficult language used by Bourdieu and problems of translation even acknowledged by his English translator (Nice 1997) his concepts of 'cultural capital' and 'habitus' were popular amongst some researchers as explanations of findings which appeared to demonstrate social (especially *class*) reproduction.

However, although widely cited by contemporary researchers, the use of the concepts of 'habitus' and 'cultural capital' to explain differences in individuals' choice behaviours (and resulting social reproduction) is problematic for several reasons. In a rare critical evaluation of Bourdieu's use of the term Sullivan's (2002a, p. 144) careful analysis reveals that 'the concept of habitus is theoretically incoherent and has no clear use for empirical researchers'. In relation to the work of Reay (1995) and Reay *et al.* (2001) amongst others, she concludes that this concept adds little to the researchers' work, and 'the main use of habitus is to give a veneer of sophistication to empirical findings' (Sullivan 2002a, p. 150).

Sullivan goes on to argue that although 'cultural capital' is potentially useful 'this concept is not clearly defined [by Bourdieu]' (p. 163) and has been operationalised in many different ways in different studies. It is not clearly operationalised at all in any of the studies of choice just cited and, in an interesting parallel with Sullivan's conclusion about Bourdieu, these authors often appear 'to assume much of what [they] set out to prove' (p. 155).

Blackburn (2003), however, objects to the use of the term 'capital' on more fundamental grounds. He argues very convincingly that referring to human, social or cultural resources as forms of 'capital' is both inaccurate and misleading. The use of the term implies both that there is some kind of parallel with the properties of economic capital and that 'social capital', for example, is something more than mere social resources. Blackburn demonstrates that these so-called forms of capital share very few similarities with economic capital and display many characteristics that are completely incompatible with it. Whilst economic capital is reduced by expenditure, for example, 'social capital' appears unaffected or even increased by its use. These alternative 'forms of capital' are not coherent or useful even at the level of metaphor, let alone as theoretical constructs.

Blackburn (2003) raises a similar issue to Sullivan (2002a) regarding the measurement of human, social and cultural 'capital'. He argues that these terms often appear to cover a very wide range of resources and, in contrast to economic capital, they are not amenable to direct measurement. A related problem is that the very 'breadth of coverage . . . removes any explanatory potential' (p. 6). He ends by stating that while 'there is nothing, other than common sense and clarity, to stop anything being labelled "capital" ' (p. 6), 'in view of the traditional meaning, this extended application is inappropriate, misleading and generally unhelpful' (p. 9).

Despite these difficulties, many influential studies of post-16 choice (e.g. Hodkinson *et al.* 1996; Foskett and Hesketh 1997; Hemsley-Brown 1999; Ball *et al.* 2000) have drawn on Bourdieu's work to help 'explain' the different choices made by students from different socio-economic backgrounds, thereby offering an account of one of the major causes of social reproduction. This is particularly common among small-scale studies, despite the difficulties of drawing conclusions about large groups (such as social classes) from very small samples (only 10 students in the case of Hodkinson *et al.* (1997)).

There is also the additional problem that, although these researchers are clearly interested in the concept of class, only one of the studies mentioned here provides a clear definition and operationalisation of the concept.

Such problems can be illustrated using an example from the work of Ball *et al.* (2000). While the authors make much of the 'classed' nature of choice in their conclusions, at no point do they discuss what they mean by 'class', or how it was operationalised or measured in their study. The two 'ordinary young men' used by Ball *et al.* (2000) to illustrate the different ways young people approach the choice process provide an example of the problems caused by this lack of specificity. While a teacher at their school had originally identified them as 'middle-class' and one of the young men's mother was a teacher, placing him in the service class using most popular schema, the authors rely on the participants' insistences that they are working class and treat them as such in their analyses (see later discussion).

This approach to the measurement of class is clearly problematic. As previously stated, it is difficult to arrive at secure conclusions about the influence of class in small-scale studies and any such conclusions are only weakened by unnecessary ambiguity about its measurement. Because of its influential status Ball *et al.*'s study is examined in greater detail later in this chapter, where other examples of similar problems are discussed.

While Bourdieu's theoretical framework has recently enjoyed popularity amongst educational researchers, other neo-Marxist authors have fared less well. References to the work of American neo-Marxists Bowles and Gintis (1976) had almost disappeared by the late 1980s, with their ideas often dismissed as overly deterministic and based on 'exaggerated . . . correspondences' between young people's social backgrounds and their future adult lives (Roberts 1995, p. 4).

Goldthorpe's (1996) 'rational action' theory, however, appears to have attracted more attention from educational researchers abroad than in the United Kingdom. Andres *et al.* (1999, p. 263), in an article documenting their research in Canada, offer a useful summary of Goldthorpe's (1996) position:

> According to *rational action theory*, people behave according to their own interest in the sense that they attempt to maximise the

> utility of their decisions. In an economic explanation of post-secondary choice, educational, and hence, occupational expectations are directly related to the degree to which economic conditions are favourable.

If rational action theory corresponds with social reality, investment in post-16 education and training is thus assessed by an individual in terms of its expected return. The time and other resources needed are compared to the potential loss of income or earnings and other costs incurred by that investment. This will, of course, depend on an individual's position in the academic as well as social hierarchy, as both educational as well as economic resources affect the kind of return possible from further investment.

Roberts (1997a, p. 61) notes that rational action theory avoids overdeterminism at the same time as avoiding a condescending view of those in positions of low socio-economic status (SES). It also appeals to a 'common sense' logic because of the assertion that 'the costs and benefits of reaching any position will vary according to the actors' starting points' (p. 61).

This theory has also been subject to much recent criticism, however. It has been accused of being based on an over-simplified conception of human action and has raised issues relating to the 'rationality' of individual actors. Whilst its defenders shy away from strong versions of rationality, proposing that students 'do not make explicit calculations of rates of return . . .[but] respond to changes and differences in initial *estimates* of these returns' (Stager 1996, p. 3, emphasis added), Sullivan (2002b) raises doubts about whether even the proponents of this well-established thesis are coherent about what constitutes rational behaviour. Foskett and Hemsley-Brown (2001) have also noted that it is often the case that any returns will only be realised in the distant future. There would, therefore, be substantial variation in the difficulty of estimating returns on particular choices and the accuracy of such estimates.

The extensive literature on school choice appears to have reached a consensus that there may be very little that is 'rational' about parental decision making. Gorard (1997) argues that parents do not appear to behave, or even want to behave as public choice theory predicts, whilst Young (1994, p. 2) concludes that 'parents and children rarely choose schools on the basis of well-informed comparisons'.

Echols and Willms (1995) offer an explanation of this, arguing that the complex nature of the choices parents have to make, involving assessments of both the needs of their children and the attributes of different institutions, requires them to make judgements based on the possession of 'imperfect' information. West *et al.* (1995) doubt parents' ability to act 'competently' or 'rationally' during any aspect of the choice process, finding that choices tended to be made along much more 'impressionistic' lines. Martin (1995, in Gorard 1997, p. 13) goes further, stating that existing research suggests that 'parents have neither the skills nor the information about schools to act in . . . a rational way'.

The degree of freedom that young people have to make decisions about their education and future careers is not an issue that is likely to be resolved in the near future. It is, by its very nature, very difficult to research. It is hard to see how progress in the area is to be made, however, when researchers appear to be so tightly bound to particular theoretical positions. For as Sjöberg (2005, p. 7) argues, if 'the researcher hopes to find evidence for a cherished theory, he or she will usually be able to do so'.

As will be discussed later in this chapter, research in the area of post-16 transitions has been 'captured' by particular theoretical perspectives which are, in some cases, of little explanatory use. The current study was conducted in a spirit of openness and guided by the principles of 'curiosity and surprise' advocated by Gorard (2002, 2004). It may be that greater progress would be made if more empirical work was conducted by researchers who are prepared to be surprised by what they find and are willing to modify their preconceptions and theoretical allegiances in the light of evidence.

Occupational aspirations

Whilst occupational aspirations are not linked to post-16 choices with the same immediacy as in the 1960s and the 1970s, the decisions young people make at this juncture can certainly affect their labour market futures. Any study of post-16 choice, therefore, cannot afford to ignore the role that such aspirations play in students' decision making. Aspirations, however, are not the same as outcomes and, as some commentators have noted (e.g. Furlong and Biggart 1999) they may also be different to expectations.

During periods when the majority of UK school leavers entered the labour market directly after leaving school, occupational aspirations and expectations were central to any choices made at the end of compulsory schooling. Indeed, for many young people choices were limited to deciding between the various areas of employment open to them. However, since the dramatic increase in participation in further and higher education witnessed during the 1980s and the 1990s, only a small minority of school leavers enter employment at age 16. As the average time young people spend in full-time education has increased, decision making in Year 11 (at age 15–16 years) has become further removed from the transition to work.

Although some authors (e.g. Andres *et al.* 1999) have argued that researchers studying youth transitions have tended to neglect young people's occupational aspirations and expectations, this assertion is not borne out by the evidence. Indeed, from Willis (1977) in the 1970s, through Brown (1987) in the 1980s, to Ball *et al.* (2000) in the 1990s, many studies have explicitly addressed such issues. Nevertheless, Furlong and Biggart (1999) contend that there is a paucity of longitudinal studies in the area and currently popular theories have not been properly tested.

There are, however, conceptual issues to be addressed in this area. Before young people's career ambitions can be properly researched, appropriate terms must be defined and operationalised. Decisions must be made regarding the precise meaning of particular concepts for researchers and these meanings must be shared with respondents. Furlong and Biggart (1999, p. 23) differentiate between 'aspirations' and 'expectations' but admit that difficulties can arise when young people are asked to distinguish between occupations they would ideally like to pursue, and those that they realistically expect to enter. Furlong (1992, p. 150) emphasises the importance of examining such subjective dimensions alongside the objective outcomes of decision making, 'both because they are not simply a reflection of available opportunities and because they enable us to examine the experience of the transition on a subjective level'.

One of the problems with studies investigating the occupational aspirations and/or expectations of young people relates to the respondents' perceptions of the job they purport to aspire to. Research into expectations, particularly, must also investigate how knowledgeable young people are about the career they wish to follow and the routes they must pursue in order to achieve this. Furlong and Cartmel (1995) provide evidence to suggest that students' occupational aspirations develop alongside their perceptions of their own academic ability. In light of this, it might be unrealistic to expect students to formulate realistic career goals until quite late in their academic careers. It would be sensible to assume that young people would reach such decisions at different times but the question of when the majority have seriously considered the matter must still be raised. As Taylor (1992) reports that Year 11 students in her study had only very vague ideas about the future jobs they might pursue, it may be the case that in the current context of extended participation it is unrealistic to expect many students to have settled on occupational preferences by the end of compulsory schooling.

While the subjective experiences of individuals are interesting in their own right, comparing these with large-scale data on destinations provides additional insights. It is relatively straightforward either to collect data showing macro trends or regarding individuals' career intentions or expectations but the 'discrepancy between individual/subjective viewpoints and larger-scale . . . structural patterns and trends' (Rudd and Evans 1998, p. 41) presents much more difficult empirical and analytical challenges. The central problem of 'the relationship between structural determinants and young people's career aspirations' (Andres *et al.* 1999, p. 261) is 'the apparent incompatibility between young people's perceived feelings of autonomy and control' and the influence of social structure (Rudd 1997, p. 267). As Rudd argues, 'the literature has still not fully accounted for levels of youth optimism . . . persist[ing] even after the dramatic rise in youth unemployment' (p. 267).

In the early 1960s, Carter (1962) found that the social backgrounds of young people were much more accurate indicators of their subsequent labour market careers than were their vocational aspirations, whilst over a decade later Ashton and Field (1976) demonstrated the enduring importance of structural factors on labour market outcomes. Evidence to support Roberts's (1968, 1977) thesis has also been plentiful in the 1980s and the 1990s. Many of the working-class 'ordinary kids' in Brown's (1987) study in South Wales failed to adjust their expectations in line with changing economic and labour market conditions and Furlong (1992, p. 121), in a study based on Scottish School Leavers Survey data for the 1985 cohort of 16 year-olds, concluded that

> occupational entry is more accurately understood in terms of the opportunities available to young people within the labour market

> rather than as part of a process in which they manage to implement their occupational aspirations.

The Economic and Social Research Council's (ESRC) *16–19 Initiative*, conducted at the end of the 1980s, re-affirmed structural factors as of continuing importance to aspirations.

> Choices are not made in isolation. The young person is subject to 'structural' influences stemming from the social and cultural groups to which he or she belongs. Thus social class, gender, and ethnicity will all play a part in shaping aspirations, as do the characteristics of the locality in which the young person lives. (Banks *et al.* 1992, pp. 1–2)

It is these four factors (social class, gender, ethnicity and locality) that have been shown to have had the strongest influence on individual career trajectories. Halsey *et al.*'s (1980) study is an oft-cited landmark in this area (but has been criticised for using only the fathers' occupation to measure the social class of a family). More recently Gorard *et al.* (1998), using historical accounts from over 1,200 structured interviews, demonstrated how multivariate statistical models can predict patterns of lifetime educational participation with an extremely high degree of accuracy (90 + per cent), using only the information available at the end of an individual's compulsory schooling. Dolton *et al.* (1999), in an analysis of YCS data (see later discussion) current to and including 1997, found that both specific qualification levels and the probability of entering post-16 education rise with nearly all indicators of socio-economic status (SES). Regardless of attainment, having parents employed in skilled or professional occupations or who are graduates, living in owner-occupied housing, and coming from a smaller family, all increase the probability both of achieving 'high' General Certificate of Secondary Education (GCSE) results and staying-on in education.

Although structural factors clearly impact on both participation in education and labour market outcomes, their impact on occupational aspirations and expectations is less straightforward. Young people's occupational aspirations are often incongruent with their expected education and labour market futures, in terms of the level of participation. Put simply, young people from lower SES backgrounds tend to be over-optimistic about their future career prospects. Male and female students' aspirations, however, lean towards traditional patterns of participation for each sex in both education and the labour market, suggesting that gender shapes aspirations and expectations to a much greater degree than does occupational class background.

Research on post-16 choice in the late 1990s

Having addressed the wider debates surrounding youth transitions earlier in this chapter, this section examines research specifically examining post-16 choice in the late 1990s. As Payne (2003, p. 59) notes, 'the evidence base underpinning our understanding of how young people make their choices at 16 is fairly thin', partly because of the scarcity of longitudinal studies. Indeed, most researchers have either undertaken large-scale, survey-based, cross-sectional studies or small-scale, interview-based studies. There have been a few 'mixed method' studies, however, that have combined questionnaire-based surveys with individual interviews (e.g. Taylor 1992).

Particular issues addressed by researchers include the timing of decision making, the factors influencing choices, and the actors involved in the choice process. These are discussed below, before 'models' of decision making are addressed, and particularly influential studies are examined.

Timing

The point at which young people begin to consider their post-16 options has been addressed by a number of studies in the area. Indeed, the timing of the initiation of the post-16 choice process has implications for the collection of data in this area. If some young people begin to consider their post-16 options well before the beginning of Year 11, data should either be collected in previous years or accounts of previous choices need to be sought. The present study, for example, found that students made links between the choices they made in Year 9 and those they were faced with at the end of compulsory schooling. Many studies do not address this important question, however, and even among those that do the evidence in this area is mixed.

Foskett and Hesketh's (1997) findings suggested that a large minority (42 per cent) of students had started thinking about their post-16 choices before the last year of compulsory schooling. Over a quarter of students had begun considering their options while still in Year 10 and more than 1 in 10 had started weighing up their post-16 choices in Year 9. Considering that the fieldwork for their study was conducted at the end of Year 11, it is somewhat surprising that half the sample had only 'just recently' begun to think about possible post-16 destinations.

Their most unexpected finding relates to social class, however. Although they are unclear about how social class is either defined or operationalised (a weakness common to research in this area), they report finding no substantial class differences in relation to the timing of students' decisions. Many small-scale studies in the area of post-16 choice (e.g. Hemsley-Brown 1999; Ball *et al.* 2000) and school choice (e.g. Gewirtz *et al.* 1995) have stressed the 'classed' nature of the choice process. While these studies have not escaped criticism in relation to such claims (see Gorard 1997; Payne 2003; White 2007), Foskett and Hesketh's (1997) finding questions the influence of class on at least one aspect of the choice process. The relatively large scale of their study serves to strengthen their case.

While their study certainly provides the most detailed analysis of the timing of students' post-16 decisions, there are aspects of Foskett and Hesketh's (1997) findings that are confusing. They initially state, for example, that 40 per cent of their sample had 'always known' their post-16 intentions but, in relation to another question, only 19 per cent of students report having 'always known' what they were going to do at the end of Year 11. Additionally, if either 40 per cent or even 19 per cent of students had indeed 'always known' their post-16 intentions, it would be expected that a larger proportion than the 5 per cent they reported would have thought about their choices before Year 9.

This anomaly in the analysis appears to reflect misunderstandings or inconsistencies on the part of students, but it does mar what would otherwise have been compelling evidence from a relatively large study (n = 1284) with an impressively high response rate (90 per cent). Treated cautiously, however, this study still provides the most robust data in relation to the timing of students' choices.

Hemsley-Brown's (1999) findings from a much smaller scale study (with a sample of 25 students) provide a potential resolution to the students' apparent confusion about when they actually started thinking about their post-16 options. She argues that although most students had not made firm decisions about specific post-16 destinations until at least Year 10, many held long-standing ideas about the kind of courses and/or institutions that they would consider. This finding is in line with research into 'school choice' where some researchers (e.g. Gorard 1997) have reported that parents knew what 'kind' of school they wanted their child to attend long before they had made decisions relating to particular institutions. Indeed, Gorard (1997) suggests that the time scale over which educational decisions are made has probably been underestimated by most researchers in the area.

While students' decisions relating to their immediate post-16 destinations may vary, Taylor's (1992) research suggests that most young people had only very vague ideas about the occupations they would like to pursue eventually. This may not be surprising, given the extended transition to the labour market that young people now face (Furlong and Cartmel 1997), but is important in relation to the present discussion. It suggests, perhaps, that the point at which young people begin thinking about their immediate post-16 destinations is not necessarily the point at which they also start thinking about their labour market futures.

The timing of young people's decision making is a difficult topic to research. Researchers must rely on students' accounts, and it is not clear whether the students themselves are able to pinpoint exactly when they began thinking about their post-16 options. The distinction between thinking about such options in *general*, at the level of what kinds of destination would at least warrant consideration, and deciding about *specific* institutions and courses complicates the matter further.

Factors influencing individual decisions

Choices relating to post-16 destinations can be divided, at least theoretically, into four areas. The first decision facing students is whether to 'stay-on' in post-16 education and/or training, or to seek work. Students deciding to continue their education must then make decisions relating to qualification types, subjects and institutions. However, as it will become clear in the following discussion, it is not always possible in practice to separate decisions into these elements.

Staying-on or leaving

Keys *et al.* (1998) examined the choices made by young people who had continued their full-time education into Year 12. In this large-scale, multi-method study of young people's post-16 choices, the three most important factors reported by students as influential to their decision to 'stay-on' were, to get appropriate qualifications for a particular job, to gain the qualifications necessary to enter higher education, and to carry on studying. This is remarkably similar to the results of a study by Vincent and Dean (1977), carried out 30 years previously, in which students cited higher education, specific career goals and generally increasing employability as the most influential factors on their decision to continue with their education.

Many of the young people in Taylor's (1992) study valued qualifications for their relevance to the labour market but, unlike Keys *et al.* (1998), she found little evidence of students placing intrinsic value on study. In her review of the area, Payne (2003, p. 17) concludes that past research generally concurs that 'young people have a very instrumental approach to education'.

Instrumental attitudes towards education and qualifications have consistently been found to be important in influencing young people to stay on in full-time education after the age of 16 and are clearly not a new phenomenon. They cannot, therefore, be linked directly to either changes in the labour market or the expansion of the Further Education (FE) sector in the 1980s and the 1990s. However, the dramatic increase in the proportion of young people entering post-16 education and training during that period has meant that more school leavers now face decisions relating to post-16 education and training. In the following discussion, factors relating to choice of institutions and courses are considered.

Institutional choice

As Payne (2003) notes, further education institutions are by no means a homogeneous group and cater for different types of students. Further Education [FE] colleges tend to offer a broader range of vocational courses and often have links with work-based training schemes. In contrast, school sixth forms and sixth-form colleges usually have a larger proportion of students studying for academic qualifications (see Chapter 3).

It is often the case, therefore, that institutional and course choice are difficult, or impossible, to separate. Taylor (1992), Foskett and Hesketh (1997) and Keys *et al.* (1998) all found that post-16 institutions were often chosen because of the provision of particular courses. Given both the plausibility of this link, and the range of settings and methods used in these studies, it is difficult to doubt the importance of these structural constraints on the choices made by young people.

Several other factors relating to academic issues have also been reported as pertinent to institutional choice. Foskett and Hesketh (1997) found that students often considered the 'academic reputations' of the schools and colleges in their local area. This is certainly interesting and plausible, although the concept of 'reputation' does raise some difficult issues. The extent of any consensus regarding the relative standing of institutions is not explored by the authors, for example, and the sources of information (if any) used by students to make judgements in this area are also unclear. Although the authors claim that students' views were 'based on examination results' (p. 312) it is not made explicit exactly what data were used and by whom. Given the findings of research into 'school choice' (see: Gorard 1997 for a useful summary) it appears unlikely that many students (or their parents) would engage in a detailed analysis of past examination scores.

Most previous research would suggest that judgements about 'reputation' would be made on the basis of much less sophisticated distinctions or information passed through informal networks. Because of the greater proportion of vocational students, FE colleges tend to have a student intake with lower average GCSE results than either sixth-form colleges or school sixth forms (Payne 2001b). It is perhaps more plausible that the impressionistic or anecdotal profiles of the student intake of different institutions were used as 'proxy' indicators of their academic performance, leading young people to rank institutions accordingly. Either way, this is certainly an issue that would benefit from further investigation.

Students' desire to stay at or close to their present institutions was found to be important amongst Hesketh and Foskett's (1997) sample, and Payne (2003), reviewing literature in the area, concludes that the simplest course of action is usually for students to 'stay put'. Even when students do change institutions voluntarily, however, they do not tend to move far from their homes. Indeed, proximity is a theme that recurs in the school choice literature (see later discussion) and has been linked by parents to issues of 'security'.

Given national trends (see Chapter 3) it would be easy to suggest a tendency towards inertia amongst students, who are often reluctant to change institutions. However, the fact that many young people choose to remain at their present school by no means indicates that they have not considered alternative options. As Payne (2003) has argued, there are many compelling reasons not to change institutions, such as continuity and travel considerations.

Many commentators have stressed the importance of viewing choice as a process operating over time. A related problem for researchers is that the reasons provided by students for choosing institutions may also have a temporal dimension. In a longitudinal study, Hemsley-Brown (1999) observed that while students provided coherent reasons for preferring particular institutions, they often made choices that did not match their original rationales. This might be interpreted as evidence of unreliability among students' responses but, alternatively, could simply indicate that they had changed their priorities in the intervening period. Whatever the explanation, it highlights an issue that has implications for the interpretation of data not only pertaining to the choice of institutions, but also all other decisions relating to the post-16 transition.

Course choice

It has already been argued that, in reality, course choice cannot always be separated from choice of institution, as some courses are only offered by particular institutions. Neither is it always possible to separate subject choices with decisions about qualification type. This is an area, however, where empirical evidence appears to be quite limited, with most research focusing solely on the decision to take either academic and/or vocational qualifications.

The relationship between the social background of young people and their choice of course or qualification has been explored by a number of researchers, often employing multivariate analysis in order to separate the influence of socio-economic status (SES) from ability. It is well established that while female students are less likely than males to enter work-based training, they are more likely to take vocational qualifications at school or college. Payne's (2001b) analysis of YCS data, however, demonstrates that this remains the case even when controlling for other variables, such as attainment at GCSE and family background. In similar analyses, students whose parents had 'unskilled' or 'semi-skilled' jobs were also shown to be over-represented on vocational courses. In relation to higher education choice Van de Werfhort *et al.* (2003), in a multivariate analysis of 1958 Birth Cohort data, found that ability, gender and class all impacted independently on the subjects students decided to study. Students who were better at reading than mathematics at age 11 and/or 16 were more likely to follow arts and social science subjects, and those who performed better in mathematics were more likely to choose engineering, science, medicine or law. Gender was found to have a strong impact on HE subject choices over and above any differences in ability, with women less likely to take science courses. There were also class-based differences, but these were limited to students from professional classes being slightly more likely to study medicine and law compared to those from unskilled manual backgrounds. As the authors note, however, the data used in Van de Werfhort *et al.*'s (2003) study are for a cohort that would have entered higher education in the mid-to late 1970s. As the higher education system has changed dramatically since that time, analyses of contemporary data may produce very different results.

Although several studies have identified relationships between the choice of qualifications and course and social characteristics (also see Cheng 1995) fewer have provided robust explanations of these patterns, with Fitz-Gibbon's (1997) large-scale study being a notable exception. She reports that students tended to justify their choice of vocational courses in terms of interest in particular subjects, and a preference for the modes of assessment and styles of learning that were employed. She also found that, perhaps surprisingly, a large minority of students taking vocational courses intended to continue on to higher education. Vocational courses, such as General National Vocational Qualification (GNVQ), have traditionally been taken by students with lower GCSE results than those taking A-levels. However, most higher education institutions accept students with vocational qualifications and, as Fitz-Gibbon's (1997) research showed, many students take these courses with the intention of continuing their education as undergraduates.

Since Fitz-Gibbon's and the present research was conducted, however, the distinction between academic and vocational qualifications has become less clear. Since the introduction of 'Curriculum 2000' (QCA 2000), students have been able to take 'vocational' A-levels, thus weakening the previous division between A-levels and vocational qualifications in general.

As has already been noted, much of the research into choice of qualification has focused on the distinction between academic and vocational courses. Most of the research into choice of subjects, however, has tended to concentrate on patterns of participation by male and female students, and the possible explanations for the remarkably stable trends in relation to 'gendered' subject choice. As will be explored through an examination of cross-sectional data in Chapter 3, subject choice has followed traditionally 'gendered' patterns for many decades. While the existence of these differences is uncontested, little progress has been made in terms of their explanation.

There would appear to be some, albeit limited, consensus about the factors that are influential in students' decision making. Instrumental attitudes towards the value of education are clearly important in terms of the initial choice to stay on in post-16 education, and this seems to have been the case for many years. Institutional choices are often linked to the availability of particular courses but the 'reputation' of an institution may also be important. Vocational courses are taken by students with lower average GCSE results than those taking academic courses, and tend to be chosen because of their specialist subject matter or learning style. They are, however, also taken by students who have ambitions to enter higher education. 'Gendered' patterns of subject choice and occupational preference have been well established for many years but it is less clear why these patterns resist changes to the social and economic structures.

Sources of information and/or influence

Although some researchers differentiate between sources of information and sources of influence relating to post-16 decisions, it is difficult in practice to separate the two. Information can influence a decision and actors can exercise their influence using information. Foskett and Hesketh (1997) distinguish between actors or events that acted as 'catalysts' to *initiate* thinking about post-16 options, and the actors involved in actually *taking* decisions, but it is not clear whether young people (or even adults) can think in these terms.

Perhaps a more useful distinction is between 'formal' and 'informal' sources of information. Several researchers (e.g. Foskett and Hesketh 1997; Taylor 1992) have used these terms to differentiate between information that has come from careers teachers or careers officers ('formal' sources) and that provided by parents or friends ('informal' sources).

Parents

Parents and other family members are widely reported by young people as being influential on their post-16 choices. Biggart *et al.* (2004), in an analysis of Scottish School Leavers Survey (SSLS) data, report that parents were not only the most commonly used sources of guidance but were also rated by students as the best sources of advice. Approximately two-thirds of Taylor's (1992) sample (n = 1,355) had consulted with their families about their post-16 choices, and two-fifths of all students cited their family as the most important influence on their choice. Foskett and Hesketh (1997) make a finer distinction between the influence of parents and their actual involvement in any final decisions. While parents were the most commonly reported 'catalyst' for initiating the choice process, the majority of their sample (77 per cent) reported that decisions were ultimately their own. Only 21 per cent of students claimed that their choice was made collaboratively with their parents and, perhaps surprisingly, around 2 per cent of respondents stated that their parents 'were the main drivers behind their actual decisions' (p. 307).

These findings are in line with their expectations 'that the parent will dominate the partnership in relation to decisions at age 5 or 11 but as the pupil becomes older so his or her influence increases' (Foskett and Hesketh 1997, p. 307). However, they conclude that whether consciously or otherwise, students make decisions within 'frames of reference defined by their parents' (p. 308). This claim is in line with Payne's (2003, p. 30) conclusion that parental influence can take several forms and 'parents can have a pervasive influence to shaping young people's attitudes to education over a long period of time', and there are similarities here both to Hodkinson *et al.*'s (1996) 'horizons for action' and Gorard's (1997) idea of 'choice sets'. There is clearly some agreement that young people may not recognise such influences and the implication that this may lead to the under-reporting of parental involvement. Regardless, that parental involvement is important, at least at the stage of initiating or discussing choices, appears to be well established.

Some researchers have attempted to differentiate between the roles played by different family members during the process of decision making. While David *et al.* (1994) and Reay and Ball (1998) both claim that mothers tend to be central figures in the choice of secondary schools, Brooks (2004) argues that fathers are more involved in decisions relating to higher education. In relation to the post-16 transition, Foskett and Hemsley-Brown (2001) provide a more sophisticated analysis and present evidence to suggest that there is a common division of labour, with mothers and fathers taking different roles.

Friends

The evidence on the role played by friends and peers is in shorter supply and less conclusive than that relating to parental and familial influence. It is also an area that may be intrinsically difficult to research. In relation to the findings discussed in the previous section, Foskett and Hesketh (1997) note that it is unlikely that young people would report that their parents had made the decision about their post-16 destinations for them, even if this had been the case. Any such admission would reveal a lack of autonomy that may arouse feelings of shame or embarrassment. Similarly, it might be expected that students under-report the extent to which they acted on advice given by their friends. Respondents may perceive that relying on guidance provided by peers would be viewed as 'inappropriate' by members of the educational establishment, such as a researcher, and so be reluctant to admit having done so. This would hinder any investigation into the role played by friends and peers, yet would remain undetected in research findings.

In terms of the decision to stay in education, analyses of large-scale data sets reveal some interesting findings. Using YCS data, Cheng (1995) found that the staying-on rate of previous cohorts of students at 11–18 schools was a good predictor of future rates of post-16 participation and Payne (2003) reports that YCS data provide evidence to suggest that young people are more likely to continue into post-16 education if their schoolmates are staying on. Similarly, Thomas *et al.* (2002) note a correlation between boys' intentions to continue with post-16 education and the proportion of their year group also planning to stay on. This relationship, however, was not apparent among the same cohorts of girls. Whether these trends actually result from any kind of 'peer influence', however, is less clear. An equally plausible explanation would be some kind of 'institutional culture' which could be based around staff and/or student attitudes and behaviour.

In terms of the role played by friends in the provision of information and/or guidance, the evidence is less clear. While Taylor (1992) reports that friends were used as a source of information by many of the students in her research, Hesketh and Foskett (1997) do not mention peers as an important source of information. In relation to higher education choice Brooks (2003) claimed that students rarely discussed choices with their peer group. However, her very small sample (n=15) means that generalising from her research may be extremely misleading.

Establishing the degree to which friends and peers are involved in any stage of decision making is fraught with difficulties. While there are clearly relationships between rates of staying-on in particular institutions and the chances of individuals continuing their education, it is certainly not the case that any causal links have been established. The results of larger-scale studies, such as those conducted by Taylor (1992) and Hesketh and Foskett (1997), are not consistent in their findings and Brook's (2003) in-depth study is far too small to provide robust evidence of wider trends.

Careers teachers and careers advisors

Several studies conducted in the 1980s and the 1990s have highlighted the marginalised status of careers teachers (Harris 1992a, b), careers advisors (Lawrence 1992) and careers education and guidance (CEG) more generally (Bates 1990). It might be expected, therefore, that these 'formal' sources of information and advice had relatively little impact on young people's decision making. Research evidence appears to support their 'marginal' position, with Taylor (1992) and Foskett and Hesketh (1997) finding that only a small minority of students (14 per cent and 12 per cent respectively) reported careers officers or teachers as having been 'influential' or acting as 'catalysts' to decision making. Taylor (1992), however, highlights the wide variation in careers provision, even within relatively small geographical areas. Because of this, it is possible that the influence of careers professionals varies considerably, according to the nature and scope of provision offered. As Payne (2003) notes, however, assessing the impact of CEG is fraught with methodological and ethical difficulties.

There appears to be a consensus among researchers in the area that family members, particularly parents, are the most important sources of information, advice and influence for many students approaching the end of compulsory schooling. The extent to which they are involved in any final decisions is less clear. The idea that parents set the 'parameters' within which decisions are made, however, is very plausible. The role played by friends and peers is less clear, and while current research has demonstrated continuity in terms of institutional retention, the current state of knowledge in 'school effectiveness' research would suggest, however, that any kind of 'school effect' is unlikely (Gorard 2000). Careers professionals seem to be influential for only a minority of students, reinforcing the concerns expressed by researchers in the area.

The decision-making process

As decision making is neither directly observable nor easily measured, it is difficult to research empirically and academics studying 'school choice' have addressed at length the issue of how best to research decision making. Many of the issues raised are directly relevant to the study of choice at any level and some are considered briefly before research on the post-16 choice process is examined in detail.

The 'factor/list' approach to determining the most important influences on choosers, commonly found in questionnaire surveys, has been criticised by some researchers for failing 'to capture the messy, multi-dimensional, intuitive and seemingly irrational or non-rational elements of choice' (Gewirtz *et al.* 1995, p. 6). Data of this kind have obvious limitations but it is difficult to formulate an argument against their use. Indeed, there seems to be no reason, however, why such data cannot be usefully combined with an examination of 'process' to provide a more complete explanation of decision making.

Gorard (1997, p. 63) also criticises the 'factor/list' approach for misrepresenting the choice process and suggesting that 'the choice process was approached in just such a check-list manner', adding that because the approach emphasises *why* people choose schools, it risks ignoring *how* they go about it. He highlights the danger of presenting respondents with incomplete lists of factors and also the reverse situation in which reasons not originally viewed as important by choosers are 'prompted' by their inclusion in the list.

He also cautions against unquestioningly taking the opposite approach, whereby respondents are faced with a *tabula rasa*. Such a strategy is completely reliant on the respondents' memory of the decision-making process and, depending on the formatting of the responses, may also over-represent more literate or educated sectors of society, who are likely to provide longer accounts containing references to more factors.

There are, however, weaknesses in all research designs. Although small-scale, in-depth research sacrifices generalisability, it allows the examination of complex processes, which can then be related to the individual biographies of participants. Consequently, it can produce valuable insights for future researchers examining the same phenomena on a larger scale. Payne (2003, p. 10), however, notes that a key problem with the many interview-based studies on post-16 choice is the 'small and unsystematic' nature of the samples. She concludes that because of this limitation, the evidence provided by some studies 'can only be described as anecdotal'.

There have been various attempts to construct 'models' of school choice, sometimes accompanied by typologies of choosers. For example, Martin (1995) argues that parents are involved in two basic stages of choice; first 'becoming informed', before moving on to 'making a preference'. Gorard (1997) offers a more sophisticated 'three step' model in which parents first select a type of school, then consider alternatives within that type and, finally, negotiate with their child regarding the choice of institution. His typology of seven types of chooser is integrated with the 'three step' model, with different types of chooser engaging with the three 'steps' in different ways.

But few, if any, meaningful models of choice have resulted from research into post-16 decision making. There have been two groups of researchers, however, who have conducted particularly influential small-scale studies on post-16 choice. These are examined in detail here not only because they are frequently cited but also because both their reliance on particular theorists to 'explain' or 'model' decision making has been emulated by other researchers. Unfortunately, the research carried out by both groups has key weaknesses that are repeated in their subsequent research and by other researchers in the field.

Hodkinson *et al.* (1996) studied young people who were either using 'Training Credits' to engage in youth training or considering them as an option. Although parents, careers teachers, trainers, employers and other 'stakeholders' were also involved in the research, their focus was on how young people made decisions regarding their careers. Their study was primarily based on semi-structured interviewing, with four interview 'sweeps' progressively focusing on specific issues and 'interesting cases' over an 18-month period. This, at least in theory, allowed an examination of the *process* of career decision making in a way which was not possible in the studies previously examined.

Like the 'school choice' researchers cited earlier, Hodkinson *et al.* (1996) argue that current market policies in education and training provision are mistakenly based on ideas of technical rationality and the 'belief in free markets depends on unrealistic assumptions about decision-making and largely ignore[s] the complex reality of culturally embedded social life' (p. 5). They conclude that young people do not make 'irrational' decisions but use 'pragmatic rationality' in their decision making, the latter being constrained by individual 'horizons of action' constructed through a subjective understanding of structural conditions. They replace the often-used idea of 'trajectory' (which they argue is associated with deterministic explanations of reproduction) with 'careership', emphasising the idea that young people's careers are 'formed by the individual, constrained and/or enabled by the historical, socio-cultural and economic contexts within which that individual lives' (p. 145).

The authors present 'careership' as a model of career decision making, consisting of 'three completely interlocked dimensions' (p. 3). It suggests that young people make 'pragmatically rational' decisions within their 'horizons for action'; these decisions being affected by interactions and negotiations with significant others in the training 'field'. The resulting career paths are then best understood as periods of 'routine' interrupted by 'turning points' (an idea borrowed from Strauss (1962)). This model is shown as an Euler diagram, consisting of three ellipses, representing 'habitus', 'field' and 'turning points'. The section where all three ellipses overlap is labelled 'pragmatically rational career decisions' (Hodkinson *et al.* 1996, p. 140).

Although purporting to model decision making, this theoretical construct sheds little light on the process of decision making itself, apart from making the self-evident observation that careers have a temporal dimension. In common with the questionnaire-based studies described above, the authors merely identify three groups of 'factors' that are pertinent to young people's transitions. Furthermore, two of the three groups rely on theoretical concepts developed by Pierre Bourdieu which, as is discussed below, hinder rather than aid understanding of the social world.

Hodkinson *et al.* (1996, p. 120) differentiate between the 'instrumental or technical rationality' they associate with an 'individualist, market paradigm' and their concept of 'pragmatic rationality' (p. 122). They argue that although 'the actual decision making by young people was not technically rational ... [their] pragmatic choices were rational, not irrational' (p. 123). Because the young people involved 'considered evidence about jobs and careers that was valid in their own terms' they are judged to be acting according to 'pragmatic rationality'.

A problem with this approach is that, at least in their report of the research, no room is left for individuals acting without recourse to some form of 'rationality'. The behaviour of all young people in the study it seems is contained within the boundaries of 'pragmatic rationality' and so, in some senses, the concept loses any explanatory power. This may be explained by the small size of the sample ($n = 10$) but appears to suggest that young people do not sometimes act against their own interests by being contrary, stubborn and rebellious. Delamont (2000, p. 99) warns of the dangers of justifying or even 'lionising' such behaviour, claiming that many studies in the sociology of education have, historically, been prone to this type of approach. Hemsley-Brown's (1999) findings suggest that even if young people's justifications for their choices appears coherent, their subsequent actions are sometimes at odds with their original rationales.

Hodkinson (1995, p. 7), however, appears to have formulated his own rules regarding the usefulness of his theoretical constructs. In an earlier paper outlining this model, he states that

> the generalizability of this model of decision making depends on the quality of the theory developed, not on whether the small sample of young people from which it is derived in somehow 'representative'.

The statement is clearly problematic. The quality of a theory, at least in part, depends on its explanatory power which, in turn, relies to a certain extent on its applicability to the population being studied. Its quality, therefore, can only ultimately be judged by testing it on a larger, more representative sample. In their work during the 10 years since their study was conducted, Hodkinson has shown no interest in testing *any* of his or his colleagues' theoretical concepts in this way, and it can only be assumed that he presumes that their 'quality' is either self-evident or beyond question.

The debate surrounding the 'rationality' (or otherwise) of decisions about education, training and work may well have passed its usefulness. Arguments about the types of choice behaviour inferred as desirable (or necessary) in official publications can never be resolved and have been pursued at the expense of an examination of the *actual* behaviour of those making the choices. Even when the latter have been examined, many researchers have been preoccupied with evaluating the 'rationality' of decisions. And as Sullivan (2002b) has suggested, there is little consensus, or even clarity, regarding the meaning of the term.

In order for the field to progress it may be productive to abandon use of this term to avoid debate digressing into the realm of philosophical abstraction. In the same way as Gorard (1997) concluded that there was no agreement on what 'happiness' meant for those choosing secondary schools, it seems that 'rationality' is faced with a similar problem in relation to studies of choice more widely but in relation to researchers' meanings rather than those of the research participants.

Another influential study was conducted by Ball *et al.* (2000). In their analysis of 24 young people's (16 female, 8 male) post-16 progression they claim to identify patterns and points of significance similar in many respects to those explored by Hodkinson *et al.* (1996) and they make use of the latter's 'career-decision making model'. However, contradictions and unexplained difficulties permeate the discussion of their findings.

The problems with Ball *et al.*'s (2000) lack of specificity relating to class have already been noted. A further example involves their use of four young women (the 'Class of their Own' students), who described themselves as 'middle-class', to demonstrate the 'classed' nature of the post-16 choice process. Although Ball *et al.* (2000) do not describe how these women were categorised, their parents (see later) all work in what Eriksson and Goldthorpe (1992) would classify as 'service class' occupations. It is reported that 'these young women attended college open evenings together, their mothers taking turns to drive the group to these events' (p. 75). Thus, they are not merely members of the same cohort, nor students in the same year at the same school but members of a common friendship group.

Two of the students' (Lucy and Kirsty) mothers are teachers. Indeed, it is acknowledged by the authors that, 'for Lucy and Kirsty, their professional "insider" knowledge was important [and]. . . such knowledge was shared' (p. 75). It is reported that one of the other students, Agesh, 'relied heavily on Kirsty and her mother for information and advice . . . [and] ended up choosing the same college and university as Kirsty' (p. 77). Rachel, in an extract from an interview, also reported seeking advice and verification:

> She said that it seemed all right and that is good coming from Lucy's mum because she is a teacher. She is a deputy head in a primary school so she knows all the right questions to ask so it was good having her there. (p. 75)

The advantage for these students in terms of post-16 choices thus appears to be linked to their access to the 'expert knowledge' provided by teachers, who are involved in the choice processes as either parents or friends' parents. As is explained below, the ways in which they make their choices shows little evidence, at least in the data provided, of a distinct 'practical, class knowledge of the world of education' (p. 92) that is separable from the knowledge provided by the teacher/parents involved.

Although children of teachers are, by virtue of their parents' occupations, necessarily from 'service class' backgrounds, it could be argued that, at least in the educational sphere, they have access to 'expertise' which is more closely linked to their parents' *profession* rather than the occupational *class* to which their parents belong. The four students which Ball *et al.* (2000) use as examples of 'middle-class choosers' appear actually to be using their parents' *professional* skills and knowledge to aid their decision making, rather than specifically *class*-based ones.

It could be argued, however, that these four students are only members of the same friendship group because of their shared 'class' background. They go to a school that, it is reported, 'attracted a rather narrow and specific band of middle-class students . . . with professional parents employed in the public sector' (p. 71). They could be seen to have become and remained friends owing to common aspects of their upbringing which may also be argued to be 'class-based'. Nevertheless, advantage gained *indirectly* from their occupational class membership, which is *dependent* on their association with the offspring of teachers, is clearly different from advantage gained through occupational class membership more generally. Presumably there would be students at the same school from similarly 'privileged' background who would not have access to the same expertise.

It is reported that two of the students (Rachel and Kirsty) 'showed themselves to be highly ambitious and well-organised concerning their post-16 choices' (p. 73). Rachel was spoken about by other students as a 'golden girl' of her school and Kirsty 'was considered to be the brightest student in the year' (p. 72). They were the students who, perhaps coincidentally, had mothers who were teachers. Both the other two students in this group, however, were considered to be only 'relatively successful' (p. 70) in terms of their educational experiences and attainment; Agesh was described as a 'serious student', Lucy was considered 'as above average [in] intelligence' (p. 72), but it was commented that 'in many respects they are "ideal students" ' (p. 91).

It has already been suggested that, for these four students, access to professional knowledge in the educational sphere was, perhaps, the most important factor in their post-16 choice making. It could also be the case that the two students who were considered the most academically able (Rachel and Kirsty) had also benefited in the longer term by having parents who were educators. Because of the number of cases involved here no further conclusions can be drawn. It could, nevertheless, be considered as *one* possible explanation for the differences in academic status among the four students, and one that is not explored by the researchers. What is more pertinent in relation to the present discussion, however, is the relationship between academic success (defined in terms of examination results and other criteria) and preparation for post-16 choices. It is acknowledged that 'as with the other middle-class students in the sample, these young women had done their own research for post-sixteen education' (p. 74). The 'other middle-class students', if representative of broader national trends, are also likely to be amongst the more academically successful groups within their cohort. It could be the case, however, that rather than being directly linked with occupational class background, 'sophistication' in the post-16 transition process is more closely related to academic attainment. Arguably, it draws on the same skills (information retrieval, comprehension, etc.) required for success within the academic curriculum. Of course, a similar objection to that proposed earlier could be raised: that is, that access to the 'privileges' which go hand-in-hand with a 'middle-class upbringing' make it much more likely for a student to become academically successful in the first place. But that is a different argument.

Similar problems are encountered in Ball *et al.*'s (2000) analysis of the cases of Luke and Jordan, who were discussed briefly earlier on in this chapter. These 'ordinary young men' are presented as examples of 'working class choosers' and the authors argue that this is reflected in the fact that their families 'were not concerned at all about subject choice and did not see this as an issue' (Ball *et al.* 2000, p. 98). However, in an extract from an interview with one of the students (Jordon), who talked about the reasons why he decided to take A-levels:

> Because I need two A-levels to join the RAF when I leave and it doesn't matter what the A-levels are in anyway. In St Faith's I was going to choose the ones I liked, but any ones would do, frankly. (p. 99)

An alternative interpretation is that Jordan (and his parents) only considered the factors which were important in relation to his chosen career trajectory – in this case the choice of qualification type. Far from 'not choosing' (p. 99), not being aware of 'subtle distinctions' (p. 98) or being involved in 'a very different type of choosing' (p. 99) compared to the 'Class of Their Own' students (cited earlier), Jordan merely had different goals. Although these goals required less complex decisions to be made, it does not automatically follow that Jordan made 'unplanned' choices or 'avoided making choices altogether' (p. 99). Indeed, it would be strange if students made their choices more complicated than was necessary.

Luke, on the other hand, has perhaps more in common with the 'Class of Their Own' (COTO) students than he does with Jordan. His mother is a primary school teacher, he aimed for (and was later accepted onto) a place at university and he eventually obtained better A-level results (two 'A' grades) than at least one of the COTO students. It is reported that 'within his family there had always been this expectation that he was going to do a degree' (p. 101). He is certainly more similar to the COTO young women in terms of his occupational class background than he is to Jordan, whose father is a postman and whose mother in unemployed. The basis upon which he has been classified as a working class, 'ordinary male' (p. 104) is unclear.

It is difficult to rely on any conclusions from this study when there appear to be so many problems even with the small number of cases and interview extracts that were chosen to best illustrate Ball *et al.*'s (2000) findings. Apart from the carelessness with regard to defining and measuring social class, perhaps the major weakness was attempting to find robust evidence of class differences in such a small sample. Through a rather thoughtless approach to data analysis, one of the most expensive and high profile studies of post-16 progression in recent times has missed an opportunity to further illuminate this difficult area.

Another notable recent study was conducted by Hemsley-Brown (1999). While she has clearly been influenced by the approaches taken by Hodkinson *et al.* (1996) and Ball *et al.* (2000) her work takes a different approach in terms of analysis. She identifies two distinct 'stages' of decision making, the 'preliminary search stage' and the 'refined search stage'. This is similar to the approach taken by some researchers working in the area of 'school choice' (cited earlier) and also the analysis of the data in the present study. This is important as it represents an attempt to introduce a genuine element of process into post-16 decision making. As discussed previously, while other studies claim to document such a process, they conceptualise it using terms that are ill-suited to the ideas of transition and progress.

A problem shared by much small-scale research relates to generalisations about social groups. While most such studies have very few participants, with samples of less than 30 being common, many researchers appear adamant that their evidence base is sufficiently strong for generalisations to be made. Despite the lack of clarity about both definitions of class categories and their operationalisation and measurement, most of the studies reviewed in this chapter claim to have found class-based patterns in their data. As Payne (2003, p. 60) has noted,

> there is sometimes a danger of assuming that findings that are based on a few arbitrarily chosen young people, observed in very particular circumstances, are generally true and firmly established, when the evidence base is in reality very slender.

She argues for a 'more systematic approach to qualitative work' (Payne 2003, p. 60), although this obviously includes paying close attention to the collection and analysis of data, sampling is a central concern. Most important, however, may be the ambitions of the researchers in terms of the generalisability of any findings.

Summary

A number of important issues have been raised during this review. While debates around the conceptualisation of youth transitions had continued for much of the last half of the twentieth century, the issue of the relative importance of 'structure' and 'agency' has not been satisfactorily resolved. Nor does it appear likely that it will be in the near future. Although progress has been made in identifying the aspects of young people's social backgrounds that can be seen to impact on their future trajectories when examined at an aggregate level, such models cannot account for those who succeed 'against the odds'.

Many researchers appear to be bound to (or by) particular theoretical approaches, and this may hinder the progress of the field. As Sjöberg (2005, p. 713) has argued, 'if the terrain and the map do not match, the map should be questioned, not the terrain'. Unfortunately, the theories in question are not falsifiable in the conventional sense, and always appear to be able to accommodate contradictory findings. This inevitably weakens any claims to explanatory power to which they may lay claim. Recent research into educational choice has claimed to have found Bourdieu's (1977, 1986) theoretical constructs helpful but, as the preceding discussions have demonstrated, they appear to have hindered rather than helped progress in the area.

Post-16 choice cannot be separated from young people's occupational aspirations and expectations but it is unclear how closely these are linked. While the increased participation in both further and higher education might have been expected to lead to an increase in instrumental attitudes to education, these were common many years before these changes. There seems to be a limited consensus that students are more likely to have considered their post-sixteen destinations by Year 11 than they are to have thought seriously about their occupational aspirations.

The choice of post-16 institution is closely related to course provision but may also be affected by perceptions of 'reputation' and aspects of organisational surveillance and control. Subject choices are often difficult to separate from course choices but follow traditionally 'gendered' lines. Female students are more likely to take vocational courses, compared to their male peers, but are less likely to enter work-based training.

The family, and parents in particular, are the most important influence on post-16 choices, even if their role is limited to initiating the decision making process. They may also set the 'parameters' within which acceptable choices can be made, even if their children are unaware of this. The role of friends and peers is much less clear and is an area where additional research may be required. Careers teachers and officers are only influential in a minority of cases, confirming their 'minority' status highlighted by CEG researchers.

In the next chapter the methods used in this study are described. The analysis of secondary data is addressed first, before issues relating to the fieldwork are discussed.

2
Methods, Context and Sample

Introduction

This chapter outlines the research methods used in the study. It begins by discussing the analysis of secondary data and the issues raised when using existing large scale data sets. The fieldwork stage of the research is then addressed. The selection of the institutional and student samples is described, alongside an explanation of the theoretical and practical reasons for decisions taken in this area. The characteristics of the resulting samples are then discussed, before the methods of data collection and analysis are examined.

Analysis of secondary data

The analysis of secondary data presented in Chapter 3 served several purposes. First, by describing recent and longer-term trends in post-sixteen participation it raises issues directly relevant to all research conducted in this area. Second, it provides the national and local contexts within which the fieldwork took place. Additionally, it provides background information about the individuals and institutions in the fieldwork sample, allowing judgements to be made regarding the specificity or generalisability of the findings generated from the primary data.

Very few reports of small-scale studies include anything but a cursory examination of secondary data. Neglecting to do so, however, represents a missed opportunity for both the researchers and readers to situate the study within a wider context. This can be taken a stage further by comparing the characteristics of the location of the fieldwork, and the individuals and institutions participating in the research, with the national and regional pictures. This both encourages careful reflection before any generalisations are made and helps counter charges of anecdotalism.

Chapter 3, however, stands as a valuable resource in its own right. It collects data and analyses from a variety of sources and presents a synthesis of the evidence unavailable elsewhere. As such, it provides an overview of the recent trends relating to post-16 participation and identifies the key variables impacting on young people's careers.

Sources of data

The data presented in this chapter originate from a wide range of sources that can be divided into two different types. Many of the data sets available from the government's Office for National Statistics (ONS) are derived from population data and thus are useful because of their complete coverage of the United Kingdom and its constituent nations. The strength of these data is their representativeness and they are used in this study to map trends relating to basic information concerning participation, attainment and so forth. Their weakness, however, lies in their concomitant lack of depth. These data are, for the most part, provided by the Department for Education and Skills (DfES, formerly DfEE), Learning and Skills Councils (LSCs), the Higher Education Funding Councils (HEFCs) and similar organisations whose primary activities are not research related. As a result, data sets often lack information on areas such as ethnicity, occupational class and other variables of central interest to social researchers.

There are other sources, however, that can provide such information, albeit with the drawback that the data are sample based rather than representative of the entire population of interest. Government funded, survey-based studies, such as the YCS, the Labour Force Survey (LFS) and the National Child Development Study (NCDS), have been running for many years (and in some cases decades) and include the kind of variables not always present in population data sets. Whilst information provided by the DfES, for example, can be treated as population data with a complete response rate, findings from surveys such as the YCS cannot be relied upon with the same degree of confidence. In common with most social research, these studies are not only sample-based but are weakened by considerable levels of non-response. As most government funded projects of this kind are longitudinal or panel studies, problems with non-response also tend to increase over time (Courtney and Mekkelholt 1996).

As has been discovered in previous analyses of existing data sources (see: See *et al.* 2005; White *et al.* 2006) information collected for purposes other than those of the researcher are not always ideally suited for the task in hand. Information in some areas are often either unavailable, or cannot be located or accessed. Data sets cannot always be compared directly, as they regularly refer to different levels of geographic aggregation (such as the United Kingdom, England and Wales, or just England), are often only available for the current or previous year, and when longer time periods are covered are rarely comprehensive or continuous.

The data chosen for inclusion in the analysis were selected primarily because of their relevance to the issues raised in the present study, and were considered the best available in terms of their relevance and coverage. Data sets covering long periods of time were used where possible to illustrate recent trends but, in the many cases where such data were unavailable, particular years have been chosen because they are either the most up-to-date, contemporary to the fieldwork or because data relating to other periods were unavailable.

Fieldwork

The second part of the research involved the collection of primary data via fieldwork. Decisions relating to the selection of the sample of educational institutions and individual students are discussed directly below. Issues relating to the methods of data collection are then addressed. The problems inherent to the presentation of research findings based on interview narratives are considered next, and the strategies adopted in this study to ameliorate these difficulties are outlined.

The selection of the institutional sample

The six schools that participated in the study are located in two adjoining local authorities (LAs), Dean and Green Valley, in the South West region of England. This location was chosen for several reasons. First, as much of the research literature in the 1990s focused on the existence (or otherwise) of 'markets' in educational provision (e.g. Foskett and Hesketh 1997), there was a concern to identify and study a possible 'market' in post-16 provision that was as discrete and isolated as possible. In a large city, with a correspondingly large number of schools and colleges, this would be very difficult because of the number of potential post-16 institutions. In a rural setting, however, the smaller number of institutions and greater distance separating them makes this a much more realistic goal.

Additionally, it was considered desirable that the study include as many different types of institution as possible. This was considered important because, as is demonstrated in Chapter 3, the kind of school a young person attends can impact directly on the nature of their post-16 choices. Including a variety of institutions in the study also maximised the chances of selecting individuals of different abilities and from different social backgrounds, especially if both selective and comprehensive schools were involved.

As the towns of Dean and Davchester, and the schools in the surrounding area, matched these criteria almost perfectly, the original application for funding included details on the proposed location of the research. After funding was granted, institutions that had not already granted access were contacted. Detailed contextual data on the area and the sample of institutions involved in the study, and a more detailed discussion of related issues, is included in the Appendix.

It is important to reiterate, however, that the characteristics of the area where a study takes place must be considered when drawing any conclusions from the research findings. While few areas are representative of averages derived from data aggregated at national or regional levels, Green Valley and Dean share certain characteristics that set them apart from many other areas of the United Kingdom. They are rural LAs, with low rates of unemployment and relatively high levels of income. The experiences of all young people in the study sample, regardless of their individual circumstances, will inevitably have been affected by growing up in this context. During the discussions of findings, the influence of contextual factors will be discussed, where appropriate. However, the information on the area of the study, the selection of the sample, and its resulting composition, is provided to allow readers to make their own judgements regarding the generalisability of the research findings to other settings.

The sample of educational institutions

The rationale for the selection of the institutional sample has already been discussed. Because of restrictions of time and other resources, a balance had to be struck between the number of institutions included in the research and the number of young people interviewed in each institution. Because of a concern with institutional diversity, both due to its potential impact on the students' experiences and the associated variation in their individual characteristics, including as many institutions as practicable was given priority. Having conducted pilot interviews with careers teachers in two institutions (see later discussion), seven schools were selected.

Information on six of the seven schools is provided in Appendix. As access was not granted to one of the proposed sample, Dean High School for Girls, this institution will only be discussed when it appears in the students' accounts of their choice processes.

Selecting the student sample

The number of participants it is practical to include in any study is affected greatly by time and resources as well as the methods of data collection and analysis used in the research. As is discussed later in this chapter, for the purposes of the present study, it was decided that the most effective strategy was to use interviews. Considering that all the students had to be interviewed during one school term, and based on an estimated interview length of approximately 30 minutes, an initial decision was made to limit the number of students included in the sample to a maximum of 10 per institution.

Having decided on the number of students to be included, the next consideration related to the exact composition of the sample. The selection strategy for this research project included elements of 'convenience', 'empirically-informed' (Roberts 1997a) and 'quota' sampling. As has already been discussed, the institutions were chosen first. Because the student sample could not represent the local Year 11 population in statistical terms, efforts were made to capture a reasonable diversity of individual characteristics. Having negotiated access with an institution, a request was made that students be selected from different tutor groups and from as wide a range of academic ability as possible. This was intended to increase the probability that not only would students represent a variety of different academic abilities but that they would also be drawn from the widest possible range of occupational class backgrounds (for links between class background and academic attainment see, Halsey *et al.* 1980; Banks *et al.* 1992; Roberts 1995). To ensure that the full range of experiences of male and female students were represented, it was also specified that each institutional sub-sample contained equal numbers of each sex. In this way 'quotas' were created, informed by previous empirical work identifying occupational class background and sex as important variables affecting youth transitions.

Data collection

Social researchers often attempt to study phenomena that cannot be observed directly, and this presents them with methodological challenges (although these challenges are not unique to *social* science (Collins and Pinch 1998)). Research into 'choice' or 'decision making' is a case in point. While the outcomes of decision making can be verified empirically, at least in terms of individuals' subsequent actions, the processes leading up to these outcomes can only be accessed via the accounts of the individuals concerned.

A widely accepted limitation of such accounts is that they are necessarily partial, subjective and contextual. However, rather than rendering these accounts useless – they are the only data available on the *process* of decision making – this means only that particular care should be taken when interpreting and drawing conclusions from them. They should be considered as a particular type of data and analysed accordingly. Indeed, it is acknowledged by many social scientists that such accounts, as manifestations of processes of social construction operating over time, are as valuable as other forms of data which may appear, at first sight, to reflect existing realities more accurately (Pitman and Maxwell 1992).

As students' personal experiences of the Year 11 choice process were central to the research, it was necessary to elicit some form of account from the young people themselves. Semi-structured (or 'reflexive') (Hammersley and Atkinson (1995)) interviews were judged to be the best tool for this purpose, as participants can be questioned at length and can elaborate on their responses, while the researcher has the opportunity to 'cross-examine' the participant in order to explain questions to or to seek clarification from them.

Although group interviews had been used in previous research focusing on post-16 transitions (e.g. Hodkinson *et al.* 1996; Rudd and Evans 1998) they were deemed inappropriate for this study. They have the advantage of including a greater number of participants in the same amount of time as individual interviews but whether they are the most effective method of successfully engaging with these participants is questionable. More articulate and/or confident young people are likely to dominate discussions, however well the researcher manages the interview situation. Views expressed in such situations may also be subject to the constraints of 'peer pressure', resulting in less 'desirable' responses being withheld. For example, the future plans of an individual may be either celebrated or derided depending on the constituency of the group.

The timing of the student interviews

The timing of decision making has been a subject of both substantive and methodological interest for researchers in the area. Deciding exactly when to ask students about their post-16 decisions involves a compromise. Conducting fieldwork sometime during Year 12, after students have settled into their new destinations, guarantees that all the respondents will have completed their decision-making process. However, the later young people are asked about their choices, the greater chance that students may engage in *post hoc* rationalisation of the decisions they made. Some researchers (e.g. Hemsley-Brown 1999) have also raised problems with asking students about their decisions before they have finalised their choices.

The findings of previous studies would be the most obvious starting point for such a decision but, as Payne (2003, p. 15) admits, 'evidence on this topic is limited and somewhat mixed'. Researchers have adopted various strategies in terms of data collection. While Taylor (1992) conducted fieldwork in Year 11, concentrating on students' future plans, Keys *et al.* (1998) examined Year 12 students' choices retrospectively. Hemsley-Brown (1999) conducted a longitudinal study of the choice-making process covering both years, but this placed limitations on the size of her sample.

As a primary aim of the study was to examine young people's experience of the choice process *before* the transition from compulsory schooling, it was decided that interviews with students should take place in the second (spring) term of Year 11.

Ideally, like other studies in the area with greater resources (e.g. Hodkinson *et al.* 1996; Ball *et al.* 2000; Bloomer and Hodkinson 2000) follow-up interviews would have been conducted with the students. However, unlike these studies, the intention would have been to continue with as many of the original interviewees as possible (rather than only 'interesting cases') so as to collect data representing as diverse a range of experiences as possible and to avoid, as much as possible, putting researchers' value judgements before the data itself. Unfortunately, limits on time and other resources precluded this course of action, thus limiting any data on post-16 transitions to students' intentions and plans.

Pilot interviews

Pilot interviews with careers staff were conducted in April of 1997. They were arranged with one member of careers staff from Davchester Tertiary College and a careers teacher from Portland School. These were primarily exploratory in nature, aiming to locate the academic and political debates within the context of the day-to-day work of educational practitioners. They were also used to inform the final selection of institutions for inclusion in the research.

In the academic year 1996–97 pilot interviews were conducted with eight students from an educational institution in the Cardiff area. These interviews were used to test and refine the interview schedule, and to foreshadow any issues relevant to interviewing young people about their decision-making processes. However, the interview schedules were also subsequently revised early during the fieldwork in Lumbertonshire Local education authority (LEA).

Interviews with students

Initial questions in the interviews were directed towards eliciting bibliographical information concerning students' educational histories as well as the educational and employment histories of their parents and other members of their family or household. This allowed young people's biographies to be recorded and a profile of each student to be constructed during the initial stages of analysis (see later). These first questions were also intended to put the interviewee at ease and establish a degree of 'rapport'.

As the collection of data relating to students' decision making in Year 11 was of paramount concern, the original interview schedules were constructed with this in mind. Questions about the ways in which they approached the transition were included, as well as enquiries as to their longer term plans. Specific decisions, future intentions and aspirations were explored in as much depth as possible. The intention was to elicit information relevant to the formulation of models of choice behaviour and to reveal whether certain types of choices or decision-making behaviour tended to be associated with particular motives. Later questions concentrated on students' knowledge of the opportunity structure and how they related the choices they were making to their 'imagined futures' (Ball *et al.* 2000) in the labour market.

During the first interviews with students at Railroad it became apparent that the interview schedules needed slight modifications. The primary focus of the first version was on decision making in Year 11. Choices made by students in Year 9, or even earlier, had not been considered relevant. However, during the first three student interviews, all interviewees made unprompted references to GCSE 'options' in Year 9 and, in some cases, to the choice of secondary school in Year 6. For these students, their former decisions were inextricably linked to the choices they were about to embark on in Year 11. In response to this, the interview schedule was revised to include questions relating to Year 9.

Interviews with careers staff

Students' accounts were complemented by interviews with careers staff in all the educational institutions in the sample, as well as with careers officers in the company contracted by the LEA. Careers staff were also interviewed in both a local FE (Dean) and tertiary college (Davchester). These interviews took place on various occasions during the second and third term of the 1997–98 academic year, their timing principally dictated by the availability of each member of staff and the co-operation of the institutions in which they worked. Whereas the timing of student interviews was a central concern, this was not the case for careers staff, as it was their longer-term experience of overseeing post-16 transitions that was of interest.

The experiences of careers staff were sought in order to provide accounts of the choice process from a different perspective. Careers staff discuss choices with numerous students as part of their professional roles and thus provide a potentially rich source of data regarding the ways that students approach decision making. Although neither perspective can be relied upon to constitute an accurate account of events, the two can be combined to form a more complete picture. While, for reasons of space, the accounts of careers staff are not treated to a systematic examination in this text, they informed many stages of the research process and are drawn upon occasionally.

Data analysis

The first stage of analysis involved reading student interviews and summarising data at two levels. Initially, a 'biopic' (between 250 and 500 words) of each student was written, translating the interview into a more conventional narrative format used for reference during future stages of analysis. These summaries were also compiled in a single document to provide an overview of the characteristics of the student sample.

The next stage involved a copy of an interview being coded and compared with an identical copy examined by a colleague. Emergent themes were discussed until a consensus was reached on their importance. Some theoretical constructs relating to the students' decision-making processes were also suggested and the discussion was broadened to include issues not appearing in the particular example which had been examined.

Next, a database was created and each case was entered separately. Data relating to choice behaviour and aspirations were entered into fields, alongside important biographical information. Illustrative interview extracts were included where appropriate. This organisational strategy provided an overview of the entire data set, facilitating examination beyond the level of individual cases or very small groups.

Initial stages of the analysis concentrated on conceptualising the ways in which students approached the choice process. Like Bloomer and Hodkinson's (2000, p. 586) analysis, this involved moving 'to and fro between the . . . stories of [the] young people and [the] emerging conceptual models and tentative theorising'. A preliminary two-dimensional model was constructed and later developed to reflect the decision making of students in all three academic years (see later chapters).

Once an initial theoretical framework had been constructed it was tested against each case. Modifications were made to the model when cases could not be accommodated within it and the model was then re-tested against previously analysed cases. The decision-making behaviour reported by students was eventually accommodated within models constituted of two axes representing 'types' of choice behaviour and separating decision making into 'stages'.

Presentation of analysis and findings

The presentation of the analysis in this thesis is in some ways unconventional for research which could be categorised as a 'small-scale qualitative study'. This approach is partly the result of dissatisfaction with the style more often used in studies using a similar methodology which, as Bryman (1988, p. 77) notes, 'tends towards anecdotal approach' untroubled by concerns about the 'representativeness or generality of [the] fragments' of text used to exemplify the researchers claims.

In order to minimise any impressions of anecdotalism the findings of this research are summarised using tables or figures, where appropriate. This follows Silverman's (1985, 1993) suggestions of counting the countable, endorsed by Seale (1999) as an important way of showing data to the reader as fully as possible in order to show how representative and widespread particular instances are across the data set as a whole. In addition to the benefits that such a strategy has for readers of the research, Silverman (2000) argues that quantifying data strengthens the analytic process itself by focusing researchers' attention of the characteristics of *all* the cases included in the research throughout the interpretation of the data.

Technology, increased visibility and accountability

Information and communication technologies (ICT), although now everyday tools for almost all social scientists, have had relatively little impact in academia compared to the business world. While commentators such as Coffey and Atkinson (1996) have suggested a variety of strategies afforded by 'hypertext' and 'hypermedia' in the presentation of research findings, most presentation of research is limited by the conventional formats specified by publishers and journal editors. However, ICT can play a more modest role than that proposed by Coffey and Atkinson, while still making a considerable advance in terms of the presentation of data. Bryman (1988, p. 77) has pointed out that in research based on interviews, observation and field notes, 'extended transcripts are rarely available; these would be very helpful in order to allow the reader to formulate his or her own hunches about the perspective of the people who have been studied'. It was decided that for this research, in addition to the interview extracts and tabular data incorporated into the main text, complete transcriptions of all the interviews with students and careers staff would be provided as text files on a CD-ROM attached in the appendices of the main research report (White 2002). This allows the reader access to considerably more data than is usual as well as a real opportunity to evaluate the interpretation of these narratives. The visibility of the data is thus increased, as is the accountability of the researcher using technology 'to enhance rather than transform traditional methods' (Dey 1995, p. 69).

Summary

This chapter has outlined the two main data collection strategies used in this study. Additional information on the geographical area where the fieldwork was conducted, the individual educational institutions, and the sample of young people, is included in the Appendix. These data are accompanied by a more detailed discussion of their characteristics and the implications for the generalisability of the research findings.

Over the next five chapters the research findings are described. In Chapter 3 the available secondary data is examined and key issues relating to post-16 transitions are highlighted. Chapter 4 describes the creation of choice types and stages, and the resulting models of choice that were constructed from the student narratives. Chapters 5 and 6 examine the motivations behind the students choices and, in Chapter 7, their aspirations and expectations are explored.

3
Contextualising Post-16 Transitions: National, Regional and Historical Trends

Introduction

This chapter presents the results of the analysis of existing secondary data sets. This sets the context within which the fieldwork took place, in terms of trends in compulsory and post-compulsory education, and raises issues pertinent to the interpretation of the primary data. Much of the data presented relate to the situation in the late 1990s, when the fieldwork was conducted. However, attention is also directed towards important historical trends leading up to this period and changes occurring since that time. Significant changes in social and educational policy are also noted, and their impact on the situation for students facing the post-16 transition are discussed.

Structure of this chapter: the data

This chapter will address important changes and specific trends in the following areas:

- Post-16 participation in education, training and the labour market.
- Trends in the uptake of different qualifications and subjects at the post-16 level.
- Outcomes and attainment in compulsory schooling, post-16 education and training, and higher education.

Post-16 participation in education and training

Participation in post-16 education and training increased dramatically in the 1980s and the 1990s, with the proportion of 16–18 year-olds in education or training in Britain rising from just below 30 per cent in 1975 to nearly 70 per cent in 1996 (Furlong and Cartmel 1997). By 2003 this had reached over 75 per cent in England (National Statistics 2005). This change was associated with a number of factors, including government initiatives to increase participation, changes in the qualification structure and the collapse of particular sectors of industry that previously employed large numbers of school leavers.

Ashton *et al.* (1990) argue that the changes in the occupational structure occurring in the 1980s were felt disproportionately within the youth labour market, particularly amongst males. For a number of years debates continued as to whether the decline in employment opportunities in local areas led to increased or decreased participation in post-16 education. While the research conducted in Scotland by Raffe and Willms (1989) seemed to indicate that the former was true, Gray *et al.*'s (1992) analysis of English school leavers suggested the exact opposite. In the late 1990s and beyond, however, with over three-quarters of school leavers going on to participate in some form of education and training, such debates assume much less importance. However, a series of studies conducted by Furlong (2005) suggest that *perceived* opportunities in local labour markets continue to impact on decisions made at age 16.

As can be seen in Figure 3.1, the late 1980s and the early 1990s witnessed a rapid increase in the proportion of 16–18 year-olds participating in further education and training. By the mid-1990s the proportion of female learners in this age group had, for the first time, grown larger than the proportion of males, reflecting the faster rate of increase in participation among young women. By this time, however, the dramatic rise in participation had ended, and the overall rate even fell a little towards the end of the decade. Nevertheless, for much of the 1990s participation rates for both sexes were above 75 per cent.

It is important to note, however, that aggregate data on post-16 participation often mask important differences between the types of education and training received by any particular cohort of learners.

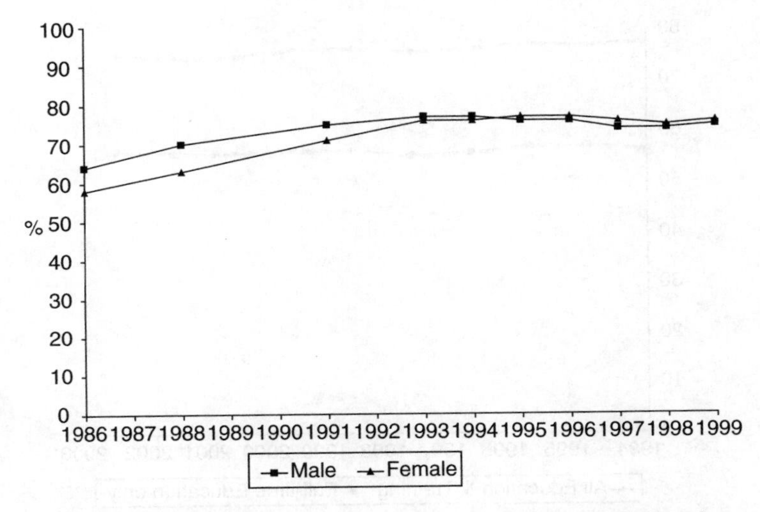

Figure 3.1 Young people aged 16–18 years in education and training by sex, England, 1986–1999 (%).

Note: Data for missing years unavailable at source.

Source: Department for Education and Employment (1995–2006).

Figure 3.2 shows that during the late 1990s and early 2000s a large minority of 16–18 year-olds in education and training were following routes other than full-time education. In 1994, for example, approximately 57 per cent of this age group were in full-time education, while nearly 22 per cent were in work-based, employer-funded, or other forms of education and training. These routes have traditionally been accorded very different status and are likely to lead to a diverse range of post-18 destinations. Students in full-time education, for example, are much more likely to go on to higher education than students enrolled part-time or those engaged in work-based training. Changes in overall rates of participation in post-16 education and training, examined in isolation and as sectoral aggregates, thus provide very little information regarding the likely futures of the young people in any particular cohort. Data disaggregated by route *within* the sector, such as those shown in Figure 3.2, are required to shed more light on this subject.

As can be seen in Figure 3.2, while between 1993/94 and 2002/03 approximately three-quarters of young people participated in some

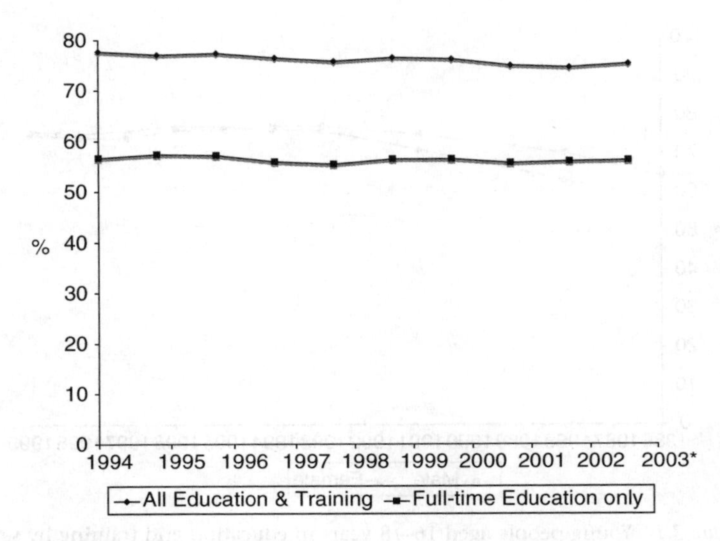

Figure 3.2 Participation in post-16 education and training, by route, England, 1994–2003.

Note: Data for 2003 provisional.

Source: Department for Education and Employment (1995–2006).

form of post-16 education and/or training, less than 60 per cent of each cohort were in full-time education. Although less than a quarter of young people end (or temporarily suspend) their educational careers at age 16, more than a quarter of those who continue with some form of learning do so outside of the context of full-time education. As we shall see, this has important implications for their future prospects in the education system and in the labour market.

Most detailed breakdowns on participation, however, only record *initial* destinations. The number of young people who complete courses of education and training will inevitably be lower. On the other hand, a significant proportion of students, approximately one-fifth according to Payne (1995), take one-year courses of education or training. As a result, figures for participation aggregated for 16–18 year-olds can also suggest a greater rate of attrition than is actually the case. Indeed, as is discussed below, even data disaggregated by year of study can be misleading.

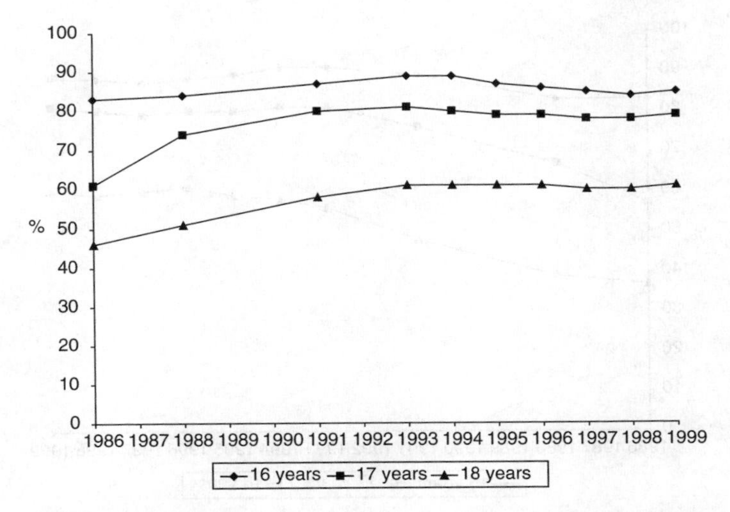

Figure 3.3 Male participation in post-16 education and training, England, 1986–1999.

Notes: Data are at the end of each year. All in full-time education and government-supported training and other education and training are included.

Data for missing years unavailable at source.

Source: Department for Education and Employment (1995–2006).

Figure 3.3 shows the proportion of males in post-16 education and training, disaggregated by age. It is clear from these data that the proportion of young men who continued their learning until age 18 is substantially smaller than those who stay on for only one extra year. It is also interesting that the proportion of 16 year-olds continuing their education beyond the compulsory requirement has remained remarkably stable since at least 1986, fluctuating by only six percentage points over this 12-year period. Indeed, participation rates for students of all ages were almost static for most of the 1990s. Any substantial change in post-16 participation during this time occurred due to the increase in the proportion of 17 and 18 year-old learners in the six years between 1986 and 1993.

The corresponding data for female learners is shown in Figure 3.4. The data in Figures 3.3 and 3.4 are comparable in terms of the general trends observed, but differ slightly in several interesting ways. During the late 1990s, participation by females at age 18 was almost

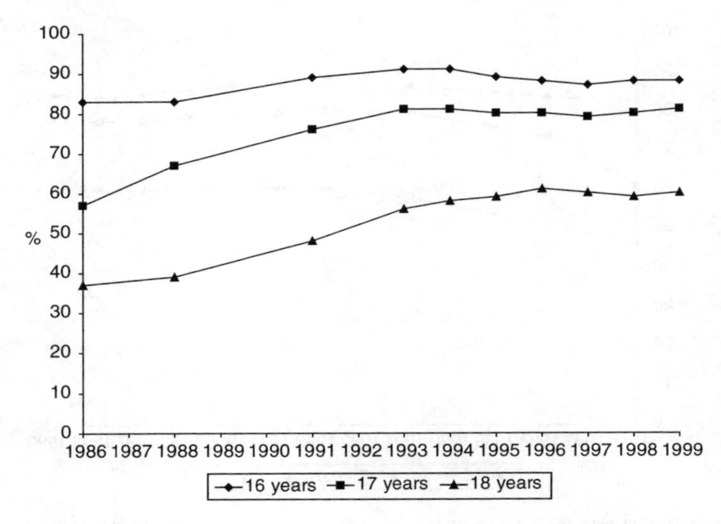

Figure 3.4 Female participation in post-16 education and training, England 1986–1999.

Notes: Data are at the end of each year. All in full-time education and government-supported training and other education and training are included.
Data for missing years unavailable at source.

Source: Department for Education and Skills (1995–2006).

equal to that of males at around 60 per cent. A decade earlier, however, there was a considerable gap in participation rates between the sexes with 51 per cent of 18 year-old males in education and training compared to only 39 per cent of females. However, by the latter half of the 1990s, the period in which the fieldwork for the present study took place, the participation rates of males and females were similar at ages 16, 17 and 18 years.

Interpreting these trends in the age profile of participants, however, is not straightforward. Courses of education and training starting directly after the end of compulsory education are usually of one or two years' duration. Knowing the age of any particular learner, however, may not actually tell us their year of study. While 16 year-olds are invariably in their first year of post-compulsory learning and 18 year-olds are typically, although not always, in their second year, the situation of 17 year-olds is less clear cut. As data were collected by the DfEE (now DfES) at the end of the calendar rather than academic year, 17 year-olds could either be in the first or second year of post-compulsory education.

Considering the data sets together, it appears that the rise in rates of participation shown in Figure 3.1 can be accounted for by increases in the participation of 17 and 18 year-olds, rather than a uniform expansion of the entire 16–18 sector. Bearing in mind the problems with interpreting data disaggregated by age discussed above, the most plausible explanation of these trends would seem to be an increase in students taking two year courses. This may be linked directly to the parallel expansion of higher education, an area that will be examined in greater detail later in this chapter.

For the purposes of the context of this study, however, it is sufficient to conclude that by the middle of the 1990s the age participation rates of male and female learners were similar for 16–18 year-olds. There were proportionately more female learners than males, but the difference was only very small. Based on her analysis of YCS data, Payne (2001b) reports that the gender gap in staying-on rates is negligible amongst students with five or more GCSEs at grade C or above. Any gap in favour of females is due to differential participation rates amongst young people with lower qualifications. While the 16–18 sector had expanded rapidly during the late 1980s and very early 1990s, mainly due to an increase in enrolment on longer courses, this trend soon levelled off, leading to a relatively stable level of participation among this age group.

Of course, the further education (FE) sector provides education and training for a much wider range of learners than those aged 16–18 years, and many of the available data sets are not disaggregated by age. These data, however, are often available for the whole of the United Kingdom, rather than covering only England. The following section briefly locates the expansion of education and training for 16–18 year-olds within the context of the expansion of the FE sector over the past 25 years.

Further education

Over the last two decades of the twentieth century the number of people enrolled in further education in the United Kingdom more than trebled. The total number of learners in the FE sector declined slightly between 1970/71 and 1980/81 but in the next 10 years rose

Table 3.1 All learners in further education, by sex, United Kingdom, 1970/71–2001/02 (thousands)

	1970/71		1980/81		1990/91		2001/02	
	N	%	N	%	N	%	N	%
Male	1007	58	851	51	987	44	2234	42
Female	725	42	820	49	1247	56	3121	58
Total	1732	100	1671	100	2234	100	5355	100

Note: Percentages rounded to nearest whole number.
Source: Department for Education and Skills (1995–2006).

from just below 1.7 million to nearly 2.3 million. An even larger increase was evident between 1990/01 and 2001/02 when the total more than doubled to over 5.3 million (Table 3.1).

Although the sector grew substantially in the 1980s, with numbers rising by nearly 75 per cent, the largest rise occurred during the 1990s when enrolments increased by a factor of 2.4 between the academic years 1990/91 and 2001/02. It is important to note that this was a decade during which participation levels amongst 16–18 year-olds were almost static (see Figure 3.1). During certain periods of its history, the expansion of the FE sector has out-paced the growth in participation by school-leavers by a considerable margin.

The balance of male and female learners in FE has also changed alongside the overall expansion in entrants. Whilst in the 1970s there was a slightly higher proportion of male learners in the sector, by the early 1990s the balance had reversed, with the trend towards increased female participation continuing to at least 2001/02 (Table 3.1). Changes in sex participation rates in the sector as a whole, therefore, followed a similar direction to those amongst 16–18 year-olds shown in Figure 3.1 earlier.

Unlike those aged 16–18, the vast majority of learners in the FE sector are enrolled on part-time courses. In 1970/71, nearly nine out of ten learners in further education were enrolled part-time. This had fallen to approximately eight in ten by 1980/81, with this ratio remaining constant for the next 20 years (Table 3.2). Full-time students have been only a small minority of learners in FE for at least 30 years and this situation does not look likely to change given the stability of recent trends.

Table 3.2 All learners in further education, by mode of study, United Kingdom, 1970/71–2001/02 (thousands)

	1970/71		1980/81		1990/91		2001/02	
	N	%	N	%	N	%	N	%
Full-time	211	12	350	21	480	21	1128	21
Part-time	1521	88	1321	79	1754	79	4227	79
Total	1732	100	1671	100	2234	100	5355	100

Note: Percentages rounded to nearest whole number.
Source: Department for Education and Skills (1995–2006).

Although no data were available that showed participation at 16–18 years disaggregated in the same way as in Table 3.1, Figure 3.2 (shown earlier) compared the proportion of students of this age in full-time education with those in other forms of education and training. These data show that nearly 73 per cent of 16–18 year-olds in some form of education and training were in full-time education. Given that some of the learners in other forms of education and training would also be in full-time provision, this figure underestimates the total proportion studying or training full-time. In terms of the balance between full- and part-time learners, the situation in the FE sector as a whole is almost exactly the reverse of the position of learners aged 16–18. While approximately three-quarters of the latter group are in full-time education and training, the same proportion of the sector as a whole learn on a part-time basis.

It is interesting that patterns of participation of learners aged 16–18, at least in terms of mode of study, are wholly unrepresentative of the FE sector as a whole. The balance between full- and part-time learners is, however, remarkably stable over time for both groups. This comparison has demonstrated, nevertheless, the need to be wary of making generalisations about FE when studying only a very small sub-section of the sector and *vice versa*.

A difference on a similar scale is evident when comparing the qualification aims of 16–18 year-olds with older learners in the sector. In 2004/05, more than half of all learners aged under 19 years were studying for qualifications equivalent to NVQ Level 3 (A-level) but only 14 per cent of learners aged over 19 were pursuing qualifications

Table 3.3 Learners on Council-funded FE provision, by age and qualification aim level, England, 2004/05 (thousands and percentages)

	Under 19		**19 and over***	
Qualification aim	**N**	**%**	**N**	**%**
Level 1 and entry	134.3	18	1,489.3	43
Level 2	191.5	26	967.8	28
Level 3	383.9	53	474.7	14
Level 4,5 and HE	1.6	>1	69.8	>1
Level not specified	18.0	>1	475.3	14
Total	729.3	100	3476.9	100

Note: * includes learners of unknown age.
Source: Department for Education and Skills (1995–2006).

at this level. Almost equal proportions of both age groups were aiming for Level 2 (GCSE grades A* to C) qualifications but 43 per cent of those aged 19 years and over were being educated at Level 1 (GCSE grades D to G) or below compared to only 18 per cent of those under 19 years of age (Table 3.3).

Learners in the FE sector as a whole are much more likely to be studying for qualifications at Levels 1 and 2 than at Level 3. The majority of 16–18 year-olds in FE, however, are aiming for Level 3 qualifications, and only a minority are studying for Level 2 (26 per cent) and Level 1 (18 per cent) qualifications. The younger group of students are also more likely to be studying full time.

Higher education

The 1990s witnessed an unprecedented increase in participation in higher education by young people. The most commonly cited indicator of participation used during this period was the 'age participation index' (API) defined as 'the number of home domiciled young (aged under 21) initial entrants to full-time and sandwich undergraduate courses, expressed as a proportion of the averaged 18 to 19 year-old Great Britain population' (DfES 2003a, p. 11). This indicator is clearly problematic because, as the numerator is composed of a wider population than the denominator, it theoretically allows an API of more than 100 per cent. It has since been superseded by the 'initial

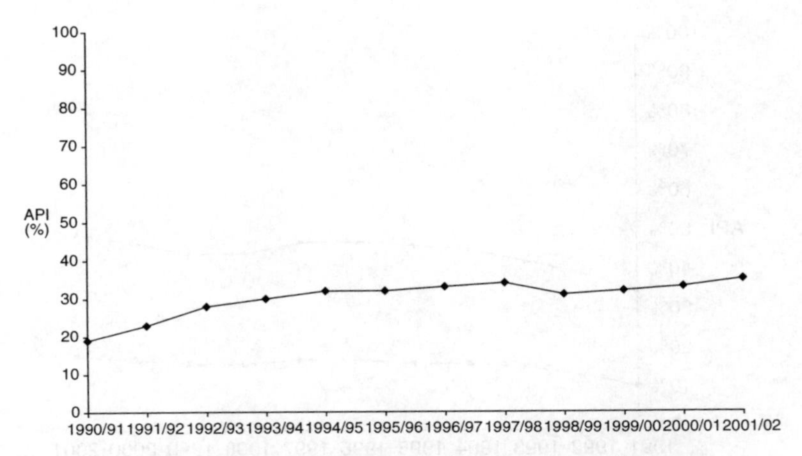

Figure 3.5 Age participation index, Great Britain, 1990/91–2001/02.
Source: DfES (1995–2006).

entry rate' (IER) (DfES 2003a) but the data in this chapter are expressed in terms of the previous measure. As Figure 3.5 shows, the API nearly doubled over the course of the 1990s, rising from 19 per cent in the academic year 1990/91 to 35 per cent by 2001/02.

Contrary to governmental interpretations of the trends in participation over this period (e.g. DfES 2003b) this increase was not at the expense of those in the lower occupational classes. As Figure 3.6 shows, classes I–III (non-manual) increased their API from 35 per cent to 50 per cent between 1991 and 2001, representing an increase of 15 *percentage points* or a proportional increase of 68 per cent. In comparison the API for classes III (manual) – V increased from 11 per cent to 19 per cent. While this is a smaller increase in terms of *percentage points*, it represents a proportional increase of 72 per cent. The effect of this change meant that in 1990 a young person from the top three social classes was 3.2 times more likely to enter HE than an individual from the lower three classes but by 2001 this advantage had fallen to a factor of 2.6.

Figure 3.7 shows the API between 1960 and 2000, measured at ten- or five-year intervals. The government publication from which it was taken states that 'the gap in participation between those in higher

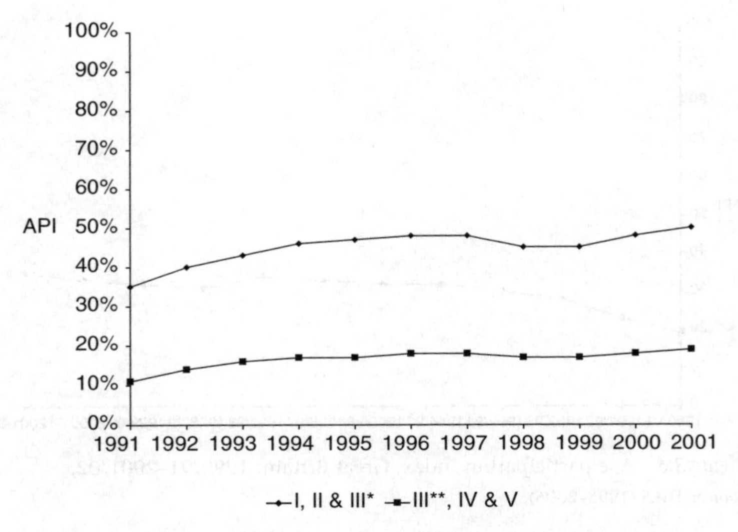

Figure 3.6 Age participation index by social class, Great Britain, 1990–2001.

* Non-manual ** Manual

Source: DfES (1995–2006).

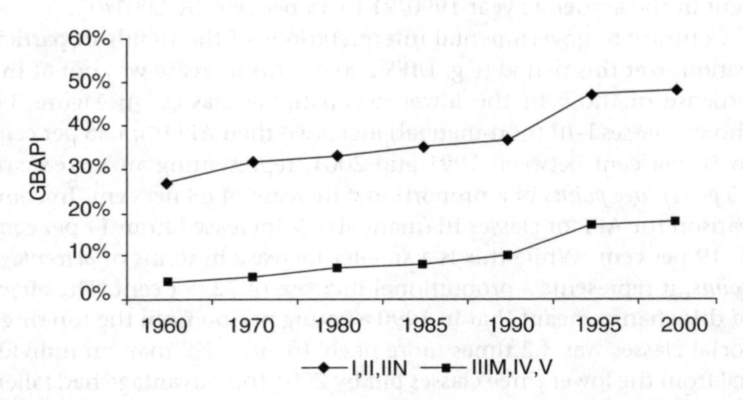

Figure 3.7 Higher Education participation rates by social class groups, 1960–2000.

M = manual. N = non-manual.

Source: DfES (2003b, p. 7).

Table 3.4 Higher Education participation rates by social class groups 1990 and 2000 (%)

	1990		2000	
	API	**Ratio**	**API**	**Ratio**
Classes I, II, IIIN	37%	3.7:1	48%	2.7:1
Classes IIIM, IV, V	10%		18%	

Source: Adapted from DfES (2003b, p. 7).

and lower social classes has grown. Indeed, if one turned the clock back to 1960 when there were just 200,000 full-time students, the gap between the two groups was actually less than it is now' (DfES 2003b, p. 7). However, this analysis is flawed and leads to completely erroneous conclusions. Rather than comparing participation rates proportionately, the authors have incorrectly compared the *percentage point* difference between different years. Only a few precise figures are provided in the text of the report, but the authors claim the data presented in Table 3.4 to be evidence of a widening gap in participation between the class groups.

It is claimed in the report that, because the increase in participation between 1990 and 2000 was 11 *percentage points* for classes I–IIIN and 8 *percentage points* for classes IIIM–V, the gap in participation between the groups has grown. However, comparisons of percentage point differences are meaningless when the proportions (percentages) being compared have changed. A more meaningful way of examining the trends, and one that leads to the opposite conclusion, is that in 1990 a student from the higher class group had 3.7 times the chance of going to university compared to a peer from the lower class group but that by 2000 this advantage had fallen to a factor of 2.7 (Table 3.4).

A quick glance at Figure 3.7 clarifies the flaws in the DfES's interpretation of the data. A visual examination of the graph clearly reveals that in 1960 more than five times the number (proportionately) of young people from the higher class group entered higher education compared to the lower class group. By 2000, although the gap in participation was still large, this advantage had nearly halved.

Concerns about class-based patterns in participation are a perfectly legitimate concern and, indeed, should be taken seriously by government administrations. That disparities in participation between class groups exist is undisputed. However, in order to formulate effective policy aimed at reducing gaps in participation it is essential that the nature of trends in participation are clearly understood. While there is still a substantial gap in participation between those from higher and lower class backgrounds, this gap has been steadily closing over the past 60 years. This trend should be taken into consideration when any ameliorative strategies are being formulated.

Qualifications and attainment

The performance of young people during compulsory schooling impacts significantly on the choices available to them later in their career. Payne (2003) reports that the examination performance at 16 has been repeatedly demonstrated to have an independent impact on the choice of post-16 destinations. Analyses of YCS (Payne 1998; Dolton *et al.* 1999) and Scottish School Leaver Survey data (Patterson and Raffe 1995) have consistently found a strong relationship between examination results and post-compulsory educational routes, even after controlling for other variables.

This section examines recent trends in attainment at school, alongside a consideration of the effects of social background on the performance of different groups. It starts by outlining differences in attainment in Year 11, concentrating on attainment in GCSE examinations, before moving on to consider attainment in post-16 education and training.

Attainment in Year 11

Recent debates surrounding the attainment of young people reaching the end of their compulsory schooling have focused on two key issues. First, levels of attainment have risen on an almost year-on-year basis for over a decade, raising questions about whether this reflects genuine progress or is merely an artefact of the examination process. Second, the differing levels of attainment of boys and girls, although relatively small, have aroused disproportionate concern about the consequences of the 'achievement gap' for both the male population and society more widely.

The gender gap

Whilst it is certainly true that girls are out-performing boys when the standard 'benchmark' of 5 or more GCSES at grades A* to C is concerned (Figure 3.8), some more numerate commentators have pointed out that this is not a new phenomena and that the gap between the sexes is closing rather than growing (Gorard 1999, 2000; Gorard *et al.* 2001; Smith 2003a, b, 2005; Gorard and Smith 2004). Others have demonstrated that although this issue attracts the most media attention, the size of the difference is small when compared to the gaps between students from different social classes or ethnic backgrounds (Gillborn and Youdell 1999; Gorard 2000).

It should be noted, however, that whilst over half of students now leave school having achieved this benchmark level of qualification, a large minority are less successful. It is also the case that the benchmark itself is an arbitrary creation and as such is only one measure of achievement. Debates surrounding the issue of 'failing' individuals,

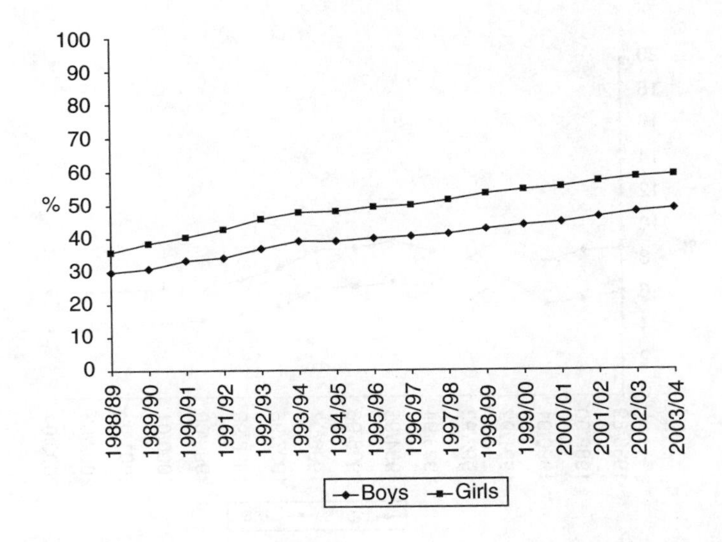

Figure 3.8 Pupils aged 15 achieving 5+ GCSEs/GNVQs at grades A* to C, England, 1988/89–2003/04.

Source: DfES (1995–2006).

groups and institutions have often focused on this particular measure at the expense of other, perhaps more relevant, indicators. Figure 3.9 shows data for the same period relating to the proportion of 15 year-olds with no passes in any GCSE examinations. It is perhaps these individuals and groups, rather than those relatively successful students, who should be of most concern to researchers and commentators interested in those who have been 'failed' by the education system. Indeed, these young people face a very limited range of options when they reach the end of compulsory schooling. As can be seen in Figure 3.9, the proportion of 15 year-olds with no GCSE passes declined overall during the 1990s, although the downward trend was not constant from year to year, and a small proportion of each cohort still leave school with no formal qualifications at all.

For the purposes of this discussion, the most important point to note is that levels of achievement in GCSE examinations improved during the 1990s, most notably in terms of an increase in the proportion of 15 year-olds reaching the 'benchmark' level of five or more GCSEs at grade C or above. There was also an overall decrease in the

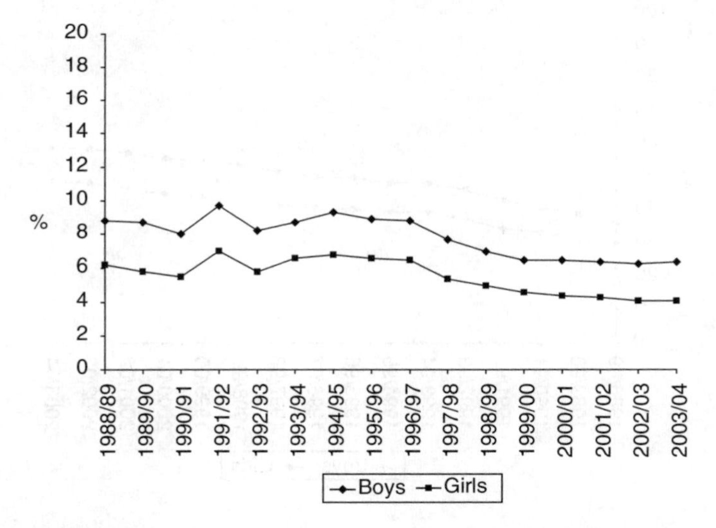

Figure 3.9 Pupils aged 15 with no GCSE/GNVQ passes, England, 1988/89–2003/04.

Source: DfES (1995–2006).

proportion of young people leaving school with no GCSEs, although this downward trend was comparatively small. Although girls fared slightly better than boys on both measures, changes over time have affected both sexes to a similar extent.

A rise in the overall levels of attainment of school leavers has implications for subsequent post-16 transitions. As qualification levels increase so does the range of options available to many students. On an individual level, this means that students are now more likely to face a larger number of possible choices. It may also be a factor contributing to the higher levels of participation on high status academic courses such as A-levels and the resulting rise in entry to higher education.

School type

Given the variety of school types existing in the United Kingdom, it is interesting to examine the differential outcomes of students from particular kinds of institution. Table 3.5 shows data on the proportion of students achieving five GCSE passes, disaggregated by both school type and sex.

The first important point to note is that the vast majority of students attain five or more GCSE qualifications, regardless of sex or institution. What is perhaps surprising is that a slightly greater proportion of those attending comprehensive schools achieve this benchmark compared to those from institutions in the private sector. Although private schools are free to select their intake according to academic criteria, Gorard (1997) has noted that the reality of the private education sector can be very different to popular conceptions, with many schools being small, poorly funded and experiencing recruitment difficulties. Data aggregated at this level fail to distinguish between the highly visible prestigious institutions that can afford the luxury of highly selective entry criteria and the many that cannot.

Data on the proportion of students receiving five or more GCSEs at grade C or above reveal more variation between the types of institution. Whilst, as previously noted, this widely used measure is arbitrary, it is relevant in the present context as it is often adopted as an entry requirement for some courses in post-16 education.

Perhaps unsurprisingly, selective schools top Table 3.5 with nearly all students gaining five or more GCSEs at grade C or above.

Table 3.5 Pupils aged 15 achieving GCSE/GNVQ grades by school type, England, 2003/04

	Achieving 5+ A* to C		Achieving 5+ A* to G	
	Boys	**Girls**	**Boys**	**Girls**
Selective schools	97.0	98.2	99.5	99.5
Independent schools	79.2	84.9	85.6	88.3
Comprehensive schools	46.4	56.4	88.8	92.3

Source: DfES (1995–2006).

Considering their weaker performance relating to the previous measure, students in the independent sector perform much better than those from comprehensive schools, with more than one-and-a-half-times the proportion of students reaching this benchmark. Whilst over three-quarters of students in independent schools achieved at least five GCSEs at grade C or above, only half of those in comprehensives reached this level of attainment.

It is important to note that these differences cannot simply be interpreted as relating to the effectiveness of different types of school. Individual attainment can be predicted with considerable accuracy (85–95 per cent) using only an individual's social and educational characteristics when they first enter secondary schooling. Indeed, there is little evidence to suggest that any kind of 'school effect' can be discerned once these variables are included in a model (Gorard 2000). The differences observed in Table 3.5 are most likely to reflect differences in student intake rather than any other qualities of particular types of institution.

Relationships have been discovered, however, between individual schools and their rates of post-16 retention. Studies by Cheng (1995) and Paterson and Raffe (1995) have demonstrated that, even after controlling for attainment, family background and other variables, relationships between institutions and staying-on rates are still evident. Payne (2003, p. 45) explains, however, that 'at present the causes of the differences between schools in staying on rates remain largely obscure', citing lack of suitable comparative data as the principal barrier to research in this area.

Although no further data relating to differences between types of school could be located, the evidence presented in Table 3.5 suggests that students attending different types of educational institutions would be expected to have slightly different profiles in terms of their post-16 destinations, at least at an aggregate level. Proportionally more students from selective and independent institutions pursue academic rather than vocational qualifications and aim to enter higher education, especially onto high status courses at prestigious universities. Similarly, a larger proportion of those from comprehensive schools go on to take vocational courses or government-supported training, compared to those at selective or independent institutions.

There is also the possibility that students' aspirations and expectations have been affected by their institutional environment, regardless of their academic ability. Although, as 'school improvement research' has found (Gorard 2000) it is very difficult to present convincing evidence linking institutional culture to the attitudes and behaviour of individuals (see above), this possibility is at least theoretically plausible.

One of the reasons that the present study included a variety of institutions was to ensure that a broad range of young people were included in the research. An additional consideration, however, was that different institutions would not only offer varying post-16 options but that there may also be 'institutional effects' at work. While firm evidence for such effects could not be established in such a small study, including a range of institutions militates against any such effects having too large an effect on the individual-level analyses.

Attainment in 16–18 education and training

Although attainment in 16–18 education and training cannot impact on the post-16 transitions that precede it, it does provide important information relating to the trajectories of those participating in the sector. It also provides an indication of the success (or otherwise) of young people on different routes. The data in this section pertain mainly to A- or AS level qualifications, partly due to availability and also the fact that some vocational courses qualifications were recently reclassified as 'vocational' A-levels (see earlier discussion). General trends in performance are examined first, before the impact of social and institutional variation is considered.

Figure 3.10 shows that during the 1990s, although the proportion of students gaining only one A-level remained relatively stable, the percentage passing two or more A-levels increased steadily, on almost a year-on-year basis. Perhaps unsurprisingly, this trend reflects the increase in the HE API shown in Figure 3.5, earlier. Comparing these two graphs also shows that the overwhelming majority of young people who pass two or more A-levels go on to HE. Given that the national minimum entry requirement to undergraduate courses in the HE sector is two A-level passes (at least for students under 21 years) it can be inferred that almost all eligible young people progress to undergraduate studies, leaving little in the way for widening participation at this transition. As previous studies have shown (Gorard and Taylor 2001), for students from low SES backgrounds, the decisive transition is the one between compulsory and post-compulsory schooling. And at age 18 the important division is between young people with at least two A-levels and those with lower levels of qualification.

As with GCSE examinations, however, the difference between the sexes is relatively small and is most visible at the higher levels of attainment. Among the smaller proportion of students with only one

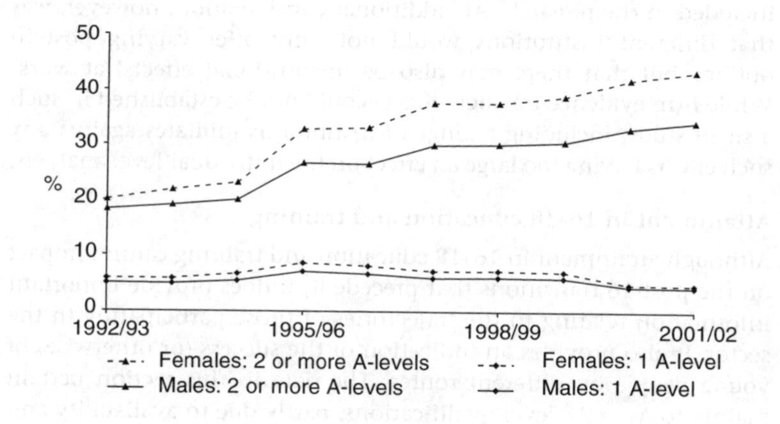

Figure 3.10 Achievement at GCE A-level* or equivalent, United Kingdom, 1992/93–2001/02.

* 2 AS levels count as 1 A-level pass. Data from 2000/01 are not on the same basis as earlier years, and data prior to 1995/96 refer to school pupils only.

Source: Department for Education and Skills; National Assembly for Wales; Scottish Executive; Northern Ireland Department of Education.

A-level, females fare slightly better but the difference between the sexes, again, is marginal.

Figure 3.11 shows success rates, in terms of the proportion of students passing two A-level examinations, between 1993/94 and 2004/05. While Figure 3.10 includes all students in post-16 education, Figure 3.11 relates only to those who were entered for two or more A-level examinations. In 1993/94 approximately 75 per cent of candidates passed two or more A-levels but ten years later this had risen to over 90 per cent. This does not directly translate into a 90 per cent

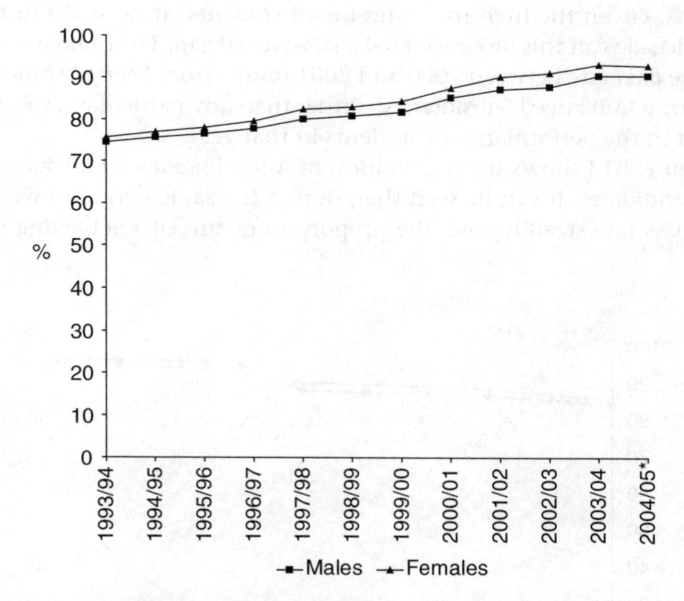

Figure 3.11 Percentage of 16–18 year-old candidates achieving two or more GCE/VCE A-level passes** in schools and FE colleges, in England, 1993/94– 2004/05 (provisional).

* 2004/05 data provisional

** Figures include AS levels, equating 2 AS levels to 1 A-level. Figures from 1997/98–2000/01 include AGNVQ results, which equate to 2 A-Level passes. Figures from 2001/02 onwards include Year 12 students entered for GCE/VCE Advanced Subsidiaries, VCE A-levels and VCE Double Awards after the introduction of the Qualifying for Success (QfS) reforms. Figures for 2001/02 show a large increase over 1999/2000 as a result of Year 12 students entering for Advanced Subsidiaries and non QfS results still being counted.

Source: DfES (1995–2006).

pass rate, however, as students taking more than two subjects could afford to fail courses and still be 'successful' according to this measure. Again, female students perform slightly better than their male counterparts, with a higher pass rate in every year. However, as was noted earlier, in relation to similar trends, this difference is remarkable for its consistency rather than its size.

When the pass rate for individual A-level courses is examined (Figure 3.12) a similar picture emerges. The pass rate has increased year-on-year since 1996 and while girls perform slightly better than boys the difference has rarely been larger than two percentage points. Given the high pass rates for all students, at no point in the last decade can this be considered a substantial gap. The dramatic rise in the pass rate between 2000 and 2001 results from Year 12 students entering 'Advanced Subsidiaries', rather than any particular improvement in the performance of students in that year.

Figure 3.13 shows the distribution of A-level grades for all successful candidates. It can be seen that, during the same period in which the pass rate steadily rose, the proportion of students achieving the

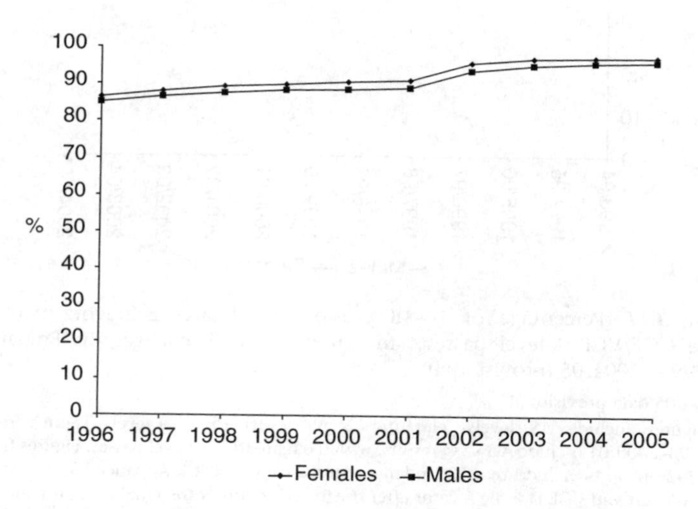

Figure 3.12 General Certificate of Secondary Education A-level pass rate (%), by sex, 1995/96–2004/05.

Source: DfES (1995–2006).

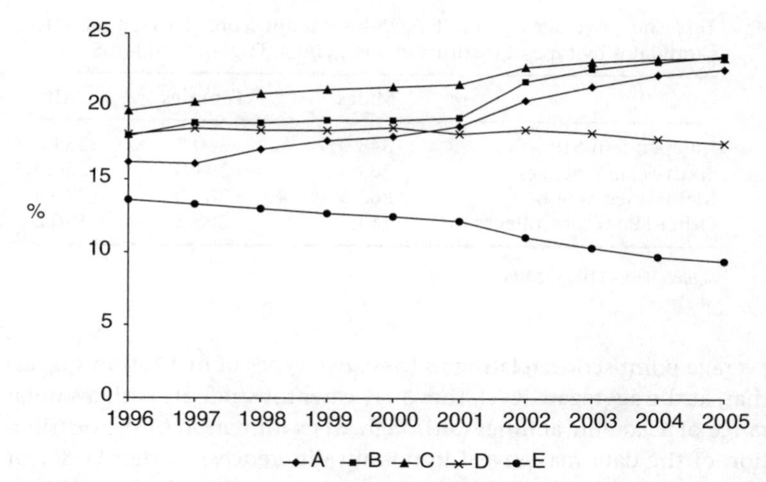

Figure 3.13 Distribution of GCSE A-level grades, as percentage passes, 1995/96–2004/05.

Source: DfES (1995–2006).

lowest passing grade (E) also fell. As a consequence, passes at grades A–C became more common, while the trend for D grades was fairly stable. It is clearly not the case that the increased proportion of successful students is leading to a lowered overall profile of grades. Not only has the proportion of students passing A-level examinations risen during recent years, therefore, but those students who pass exams are generally getting better grades.

As was the case for compulsory education (see Table 3.5, cited earlier), there is also variation in outcomes between institution types at the post-16 level. Table 3.6 shows one measure of this, the average A/AS-level point score of students.

There is a clear hierarchy of institutional types, with independent schools at the top, sixth-form colleges and maintained schools in the middle, and FE colleges with the lowest average point score. Unlike in Table 3.5, state funded institutions are not differentiated according to whether they operate academic selection or not. The 'maintained schools' category will therefore include both selective and non-selective institutions, the majority of which will be schools taking students from 11 to 18 years. Similarly, 'sixth form colleges' will encompass institutions with a wide range of selection criteria. The

Table 3.6 Average GCE/VCE A/AS-level point score of 16–18 year-old candidates by type of institution and gender, England, 2004/05

	Males	Females	All
Independent Schools	348.0	360.2	354.0
Sixth-Form Colleges	263.9	294.8	280.9
Maintained Schools	263.3	284.0	274.4
Other FE Sector Colleges	183.7	206.2	196.2

Source: DfES (1995–2006).

average point scores relating to these two types of institution suggest that, at the aggregate level, they may cater for students with a similar range of academic abilities (although an examination of the distribution of the data may reveal important differences). 'Other FE sector colleges' refers, in the main, to what are conventionally referred to as 'FE colleges' and typically have more inclusive entrance policies and wider provision of vocational courses.

When other variables are taken into consideration, however, A-level students in sixth forms and sixth-form colleges are less likely to fail their exams than students in FE colleges. This was also found to be the case for students studying for GNVQ qualifications (Payne 2001b).

The data on GCSE results, in Table 3.5, suggest that students from schools operating academic selection tend to achieve higher than average examination scores, even if this is an artefact of the institutions' intakes rather than evidence of any 'added value'. Nevertheless, it would be reasonable to suggest that such institutions would be considered high status post-16 destinations. Further Education colleges, in contrast, are clearly less successful in terms of academic outcomes. While this may merely reflect their tendency to offer a wider range of vocational and other specialist courses, it is also the case that they are often considered to be the lowest status type of post-16 institution.

Parents' education

Parents' levels of educational qualifications are fairly good predictors of their children's attainment. Table 3.7 shows YCS data on the 'study aims' (i.e. the examination level they are studying for) of young people aged 16 disaggregated their parents' highest level of qualification. The data of most interest to the present study relate to the proportion of students taking A- or AS-levels. It is clear that the probability of a student aiming for 'gold standard' academic qualifications increases substantially with the educational level of their parents. Students whose parents have degrees are more than twice as likely to be studying for A- or AS-levels than those whose parents have no A-levels. The off-spring of graduates are also nearly one-and-a-half times more likely to study A- or AS-levels than students whose parents have only A-levels.

It is clear that there is a strong relationship between parents' education and the educational trajectories of their off-spring. Similarly strong relationships have been found between educational qualifications and occupational or class background (Halsey, Heath and Ridge 1980) and it is equally legitimate, therefore, to characterise this relationship as class based. While many plausible mechanisms for the transfer of educational advantage have been suggested, research in this area has progressed little beyond describing the remarkable stability of these connections. As discussed in Chapter 2, explanations have tended to be based on untestable 'theoretical' propositions rather than on robust empirical evidence.

The interesting issue for research into post-16 decision making is whether there is any relationship between the level or status of the route that a young person intends to pursue and the ways in which

Table 3.7 Main study aim of 16 year-olds: by parents' qualifications, England and Wales, 2000

	At least one parent with:		**Neither parent with**
	Degree	**A-level**	**A-Level**
GCE A/AS level	63	44	29
Advanced GNVQ	6	9	8
NVQ 3 and other equivalent	3	5	5
GCSE	2	2	3
Intermediate/Foundation GNVQ	7	9	13
NVQ 1/2 and other equivalent	6	10	12
Level unclear/not stated	2	3	5
Any qualification	*89*	*82*	*75*

Source: DfES (1995–2006).

Table 3.8 Average point score of 16–18 year-old candidates entered for GCE/VCE A/AS-levels, by Government Office Region, 2004/05

	England
South East	273.6
North West	268.3
East of England	267.8
South West	*266.6*
Yorkshire & the Humber	265.8
East Midlands	264.4
West Midlands	254.7
North East	248.0
London	238.0

Source: DfES (1995–2006).

they make their choices. Whilst it is clear that young people from different backgrounds tend to choose different types of course, there is no convincing evidence to suggest that they make decisions in fundamentally different ways. This issue was addressed in the present study and is discussed in later chapters.

There is a limited degree of regional variation in the average point scores in A/AS-level examinations (see Table 3.8). The South East region has the highest average point score, with 273.6 points, and London the lowest, at 238.0. The South West region, where the fieldwork for the present study was conducted, is placed fourth out of nine regions, with an average of 266.6 points. Payne (1998) and Cheng (1995) found that, even after other variables are controlled for, there is also substantial regional variation between rates of post-sixteen *participation*.

Although qualification levels within the 16–18 sector rose considerably during the 1990s, differences between social groups did not disappear. While media attention has recently focused on the difference in attainment between male and female students, this 'achievement gap' has never been very large and is eclipsed by the much greater differences between students from different class and lingual backgrounds.

Choice of qualification, subject and institution

Choices taken at the end of compulsory schooling are the central focus of this book. Apart from the minority of students who decide to end their education and training at age 16, the choices faced by young people can be characterised as relating to qualification type, subject and institution. While the primary aim of the fieldwork was to examine the *process* of decision making, patterns of post-16 choices are the focus of this stage of the analysis.

Unfortunately, only very basic data in the area are available through ONS. These data are useful because of their coverage of the population but, as will become clear, they are very limited in terms of detailed coverage and important comparisons. It is precisely in this kind of area that analyses YCS data are so valuable. Because the data are collected solely for the purposes of research, they contain the kind of individual level detail that allow meaningful comparative analysis. Although the data are subject to the limitations discussed at the beginning of this chapter, there is no better data set in this area at the time of writing.

Choice of qualification

On the basis of an examination of YCS data, Cheng (1995) identifies three groups of school leavers. Those with 'high' attainment (five or more GCSE passes at grades A–C) tend to stay in education and take academic courses, while students with 'low' (less than five GCSE passes at grades A–C) results are much more likely to leave. Students with 'medium' results (five or more GCSE passes including one to four passes at grades A–C) must decide between a range of options available to them but are faced with no obvious route. As has already been noted, the continued rise in GCSE attainment means that the 'high attainment' group identified by Cheng has grown proportionally year-on-year, accompanied by a reduction in the proportionate size of the other two groups. This is likely to increase the take up of academic courses, with possible knock-on effects in terms of participation in HE. Indeed, Figure 3.9 shows that performance in GCSEs has improved considerably since 1992, the last year used in Cheng's analysis.

Using the same data, Payne (1995) examined the choices of those young people choosing to stay in full-time further education. She also distinguished three distinct routes within this group. Concurring with Cheng (1995), she found that students in the 'highest' attaining group (in terms of GCSE results) were most likely to take academic rather than vocational qualifications, the latter tending to be pursued by students in the middle range of attainment. Indeed, students taking vocational qualifications accounted for the largest proportion of the growth in post-16 participation in the late 1980s and early 1990s, with 29 per cent of the 1992 cohort studying a vocational course (Payne 1995). Those students in the lowest attaining group staying in education increasingly took additional GCSE subjects, or re-sat GCSEs examinations (Cheng 1995).

Payne's analysis raises several interesting points. She attributes the growth in post-16 participation in the late 1980s and 1990s to an increased uptake of vocational courses, presumably by those who would have previously taken additional GCSE subjects, if they had stayed on at all. The analysis conducted earlier in this chapter suggested that much of this expansion was due to an increase in the number of students enrolling on two-year instead of one-year courses. These two conclusions are complementary, as if students who might previously have taken or re-taken GCSE examinations were becoming more likely to take vocational courses, it is likely that more of these would be enrolling on two-year courses than in previous years.

Another interesting point relates to participation in HE. As explained above, a greater proportion of students taking A-level courses would be expected to result in an increase in the number eligible to apply for places on undergraduate courses. However, many of the students taking two-year vocational courses would also gain the minimum level of qualifications required to enter HE. These two trends *both* work towards expanding the proportion of young people qualified to enter HE and, as was illustrated earlier in the chapter, the overwhelming majority of eligible students do go on to enrol on undergraduate courses.

As has already been noted, in the period since Cheng and Payne's analyses, the distinction between academic and vocational qualifications has been blurred, with the introduction of vocational A-levels in 2000 (QCA 2000). However, the most important point in terms of the present study is that young people reaching the end of compulsory schooling in the late 1990s and early 2000s make decisions in an epoch when a large minority of their peers will later enter HE. Their decision to take academic or vocational qualifications, however, will not necessarily be the decisive one in terms of continuing their education as undergraduate students. It may affect what they study and at which institution, but pursuing vocational courses will not prevent many of them from going to university at age 18.

Choice of subject

Figures 3.14 and 3.15 show recent trends in A-level entries, one of the main two-year qualification routes in 16–18 education, disaggregated by subject. The first graph includes only subject areas that experienced growth in the late 1990s and early 2000s. Psychology was one of the most popular of these subjects in 1995/96, with approximately 18,057 entries, but this had increased to over 46,024 by 2004/05. Other subjects, such as physical education (PE), media, religious studies (RS), and design and technology (DT), grew steadily throughout the period. While the growth in these subjects is relatively small in absolute terms, proportionately the increases are quite substantial. Entries in media studies, for example, more than trebled, a larger increase than psychology in proportional terms. The number of students taking PE more than doubled, as did examination entries in religious studies.

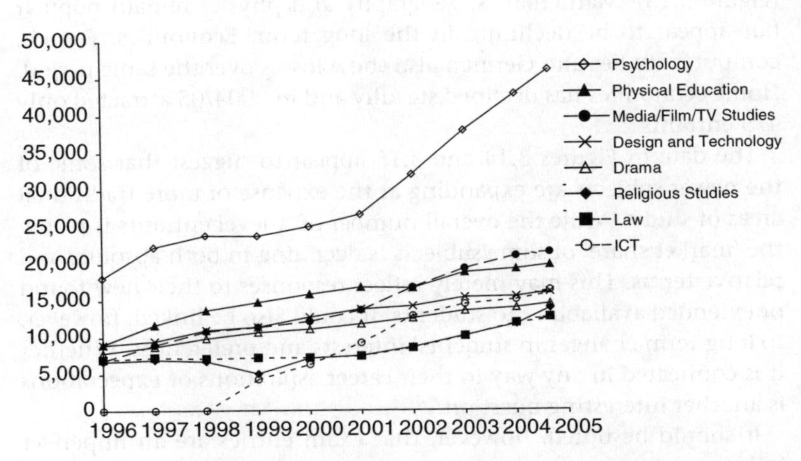

Figure 3.14 General Certificate of Secondary Education A-level entries, growing subject areas, 1995/96–2004/05.

Source: DfES (1995–2006).

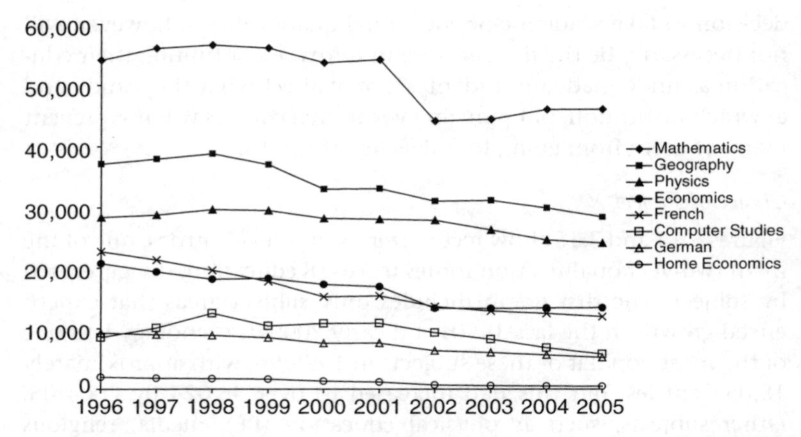

Figure 3.15 General Certificate of Secondary Education A-level entries, subject areas in decline, 1995/96–2004/05.
Source: DfES (1995–2006).

Trends in declining subjects were less dramatic than in growth subjects but were generally consistent in terms of direction (Figure 3.15). Mathematics, geography and physics remain popular but appear to be declining in the long term. Economics, French, computer studies and German also show losses over the same period. Home economics has declined steadily and in 2004/05 attracted only 475 entrants.

The data in Figures 3.14 and 3.15 appear to suggest that some of the newer subjects are expanding at the expense of more traditional areas of study. While the overall number of A-level entrants is rising, the 'market share' of some subjects is declining in both absolute and relative terms. This may merely reflect responses to their new-found or extended availability to students. It could also be linked, however, to long-term changes in students' interests and preferences. Whether it is connected in any way to their career aspirations or expectations is another interesting question.

It should be noted, however, that exam entries are an imperfect indicator of course enrolment. Some subject areas may have lower completion rates than others, and this would be reflected in different attrition rates and greater discrepancies between initial enrolment and exam entrance. In the absence of such data, however, exam entrance provides a useful proxy indicator of course choice at 16.

Figure 3.16 shows the differences in the A-level subjects taken by male and female students. Given historical trends these data may not be particularly surprising but the persistence of such patterns of participation is remarkable. The subjects in Figure 3.15 are ordered hierarchically, with the most male-dominated at the top. Very few subjects attract anything like an equal proportion of male and female students; only history and business studies come close to a balanced intake. Eight of the 14 subjects are female dominated, perhaps reflecting the slight over-representation of females amongst A-level candidates. The subject with the greatest imbalance in intake, home economics, is also disproportionately chosen by females.

Among the male-dominated subjects, approximately three of every four candidates for physics or computer studies A-levels are male, and

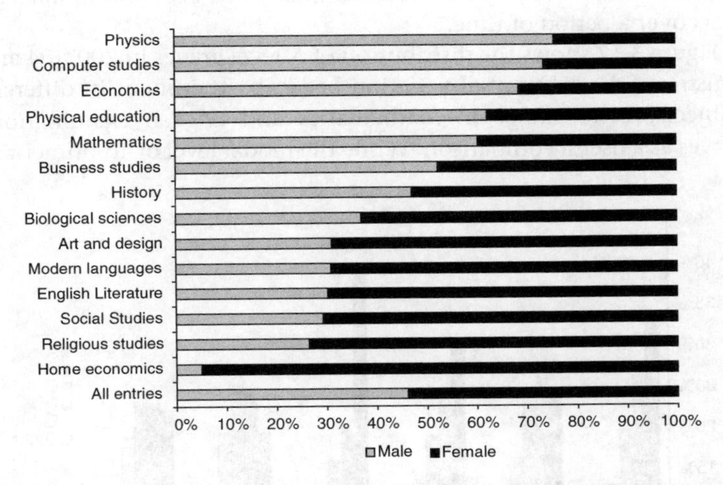

Figure 3.16 General Certificate of Education A-level or equivalent entries for young people,* selected subjects,** United Kingdom, 2001/02.

* Pupils in schools and students in further education institutions aged 16–18 at the start of the academic year in England and in Northern Ireland, and aged 17 in Wales. Pupils in Scotland generally sit Highers one year earlier and the figures relate to the result of pupils in Year S5/S6.

** Data on English Literature and Social Studies applies to England and Wales only.

Source: National Statistics 2006.

more than two of every three economics students are male. Other male-dominated subjects include PE and mathematics, although the imbalance is less marked.

Home economics is the subject with the greatest imbalance, with approximately 95 per cent female students. As previously discussed, however, the subject attracts very few entrants in absolute terms. Art and design, modern languages, English literature, social studies and religious studies are also female dominated, all with around 70 per cent of their intakes being female. Biological sciences also attract more females than males, at a ratio of around 65:35.

It is interesting to note that attainment is not equally distributed between A-level subjects. The move from norm-referenced to criterion-based criteria in assessment meant that any control over the allocation of A-level grades was relinquished, allowing the possibility of both *intra-* and *inter-*subject variation. Thereafter, the distribution of grades could vary *between* subjects in any one year and *within* subjects over a period of time.

Figure 3.17 shows the distribution of A-level grades in 2003/04 and illustrates the substantial variation between attainment in different subjects. Performance in mathematics and English examinations serves as a useful comparison. While the modal level of attainment in

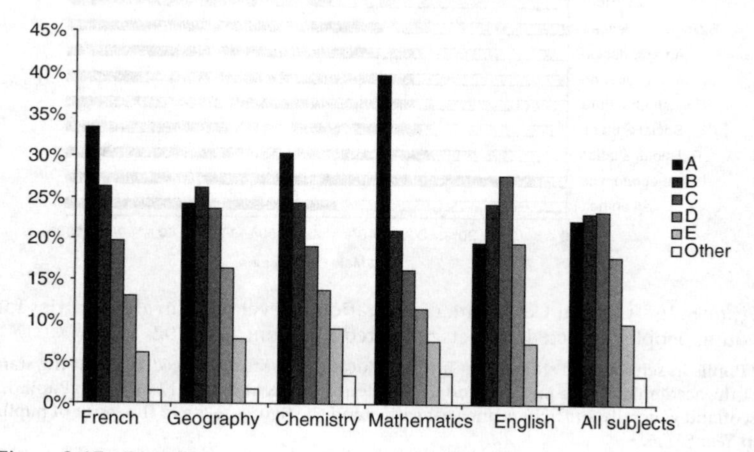

Figure 3.17 Distribution of GCE A-level grades, selected subjects, England, 2003/04.

Source: DfES (1995–2006).

maths is an A grade, as is the case for French and chemistry, it is only a C in English. Indeed, candidates in maths were more than twice as likely to achieve an A grade than those taking English, who were more likely to get a C or B grade.

The factors underlying these differences are unclear. Possible explanations range from the intake characteristics of these subjects to the relative difficulty of the syllabi and examinations. As no data could be located comparing trends over time, the extent of any longer term intra-subject variation cannot be verified.

Examining A-level results by individual subject is, however, a rather artificial form of analysis. Students require a minimum of two A-levels to enter university and many take three or more subjects. The effects of differential attainment in different subject areas could only be identified with data collected at an individual level that included information on subject areas, examination results and higher education applications and acceptances. No existing analysis of such data could be found.

Choice of institution

In addition to the analysis of course choice Payne (1995) gives a breakdown of YCS data according to the *type* of institution that school leavers attended. In 1992, 52 per cent of young people in full-time post-16 education were enrolled in school sixth forms, 34 per cent attended further education or tertiary colleges, whilst only 13 per cent went to sixth-form colleges. By aggregating three YCS cohorts (4, 5 and 6) Payne was also able to trace transitions between 'source' and 'destination' institutions. She discovered that nearly 70 per cent of students from comprehensive schools with sixth forms who continued their education at the post-16 level, stayed in the same institution to do so. The majority of those who continued their education elsewhere tended to go to FE or tertiary colleges, rather than sixth form colleges. However, nearly 60 per cent of students from comprehensive schools *without* sixth forms went to further education or tertiary colleges, with approximately 30 per cent going to sixth-form colleges and less than 10 per cent to school sixth forms. Students from grammar and independent schools shared a similar profile, with roughly 80 per cent opting to stay in a school sixth-form. A smaller proportion of grammar school students went to sixth-form colleges, proportionately, compared to those from independent schools (less than 5 per cent compared to just below 10 per cent, respectively) with 15 per cent choosing FE colleges and 10 per cent opting for tertiary colleges.

These analyses of 'source' and 'destination' institutions give an insight into the patterns of participation of young people *beyond* the more usual information on the destinations of school leavers. As the majority of young people now participate in some form of post-16 education, such analyses are valuable. Decisions about particular courses cannot usually be completely separated from choices of 'destination' institutions, as the former may depend on the provision of the latter. As Payne (1995, p. 15) notes, 'the choice of year twelve institution will often be constrained by the nature of local provision.' Choice of course will be limited in the same way. The relationship between these two decisions must be explored if the nature of young people's post-16 decisions is to be fully understood. What has been demonstrated is that 'the choice of institution for post-16 studies is . . . influenced by the type of school attended in year eleven' and the most obvious pattern in the data shows that 'in schools with sixth forms the simplest thing to do is to stay put' (Payne 1995, p. 15).

In the context of the present study, Payne's findings are of great interest. As was explained in Chapter 2, a variety of institution types were included in the research in order to investigate the ways in which young people made decisions regarding the location of their post-16 education or training. The importance of institutional preferences compared to qualification and subject choices was of particular interest, as was the way in which these three factors interacted in the decision-making process.

Summary

This chapter has examined recent trends in post-16 participation alongside the related issues of attainment in compulsory schooling and entry to higher education. It has demonstrated that a great deal can be learned about post-16 transitions by examining publicly available data sets. Much of the data, such as those collected by the DfES, cover the national population of schools and students, and can thus provide definitive, if basic, information about education and training. In addition, data collected as part of surveys, such as the YCS, can be subjected to powerful individual-level analyses to identify the relative importance of different variables as predictors of participation and attainment. In order to set the scene for the following chapters, the context in which students made choices at the time of the fieldwork, in the late 1990s, is briefly summarised below.

Post-16 participation. Post-16 participation rose rapidly in the late 1980s and early 1990s but had levelled off by the late 1990s. By 1997/98, nearly three-quarters of 16–18 year-olds were in education and training, the majority of these learning on a full-time basis. The principal cause of this rise in participation was an increase in the proportion of students taking two-year courses, predominantly in vocational subjects. Consequently a greater number of students were aiming for qualifications that would lead to eligibility for entry to HE.

Attainment and subject choice within compulsory schooling. The post-sixteen routes followed by students are strongly related to their previous academic attainment. Students achieving relatively high levels of attainment are most likely to follow academic routes, while the less successful are more likely to take vocational qualifications or additional GCSEs. Subject choices continue to follow traditionally gendered patterns but new subjects such as psychology and media have become increasingly popular.

Attainment in post-16 education. In 1997/98, over one-third of students in full-time 16–18 education gained two A-levels. Pass rates were high and continued to rise; in 1997/98, 75 per cent of entrants were successful and this had since risen to over 90 per cent by 2004/05. The modal grade awarded for most of the 1990s was a 'C' but this had risen to a 'B' by 2004/05. The vast majority of students with the minimum academic requirements do go on to HE.

Participation in higher education. Participation in HE has also increased, accompanied by a decrease in class inequality (contrary to government analyses). Considerable inequality still exists in this area, however, and students from classes I to IIINM are much more likely to continue their education as undergraduates than their peers from classes IIIM–V.

Implications for the fieldwork

The students participating in the fieldwork were located in a specific place at a particular time. For the young people who were interviewed, participation in post-16 education and training could be considered to be the norm, and the majority of entrants would enrol on two-year courses. Many of those who took two-year courses would expect to apply to university. A significant minority of students would be expected to pass two A-levels, and others would also gain 'equivalent' qualifications, such as GNVQs. Most of the students who took A-level courses would achieve a pass, probably with a 'C' grade.

The national context within which the research took place was one of high levels of participation and similarly high levels of success. Progression to post-16 education and training would have been taken for granted by many, and a large minority of students would expect to continue their education as undergraduates.

The findings presented in the remainder of the book should be viewed in the light of the data that has been synthesised in this chapter. Students' decision-making behaviour can only be properly understood if it is situated within the historical and geographical context within which it took place. Chapter 4 examines young people's decision-making processes in detail, before the motivations behind their choices are considered.

4
Conceptualising Choice: Types, Stages and Models

Introduction: preliminary theoretical constructs

As the interview data were examined it became apparent that many students framed their decision-making processes in similar ways. Although the language that students used varied, common themes between accounts were traced. With these themes as a starting point, different types of choice behaviour were identified, leading to the construction of two inter-related models of the 'choice process', one for Year 9 and one for Year 11. The categories and models were then tested and re-tested in relation to the interview data; this continued cross-referencing acting as repeated verification of the durability of the developing ideas.

As summaries of complex processes, the models at best *approximate* decision-making processes and are ultimately dependent on students' accounts for their accuracy. They represent an attempt to understand, at an aggregate level, the ways in which students made choices at the end of their compulsory education. As such, in the same manner as Gorard's (1997, p. 198) 'three-step' model, they are intended to serve as 'useful structure[s] to facilitate further analysis'.

Inclusive, exclusive and default choices

The first stage in the analysis aimed to conceptualise the different ways in which young people made choices when faced with educational transitions. This involved the creation of a typology of decision-making behaviour, described in detail directly below.

Inclusive choices

'Inclusive' choices are perhaps closest to the commonsense notion of 'choosing'. The defining aspect of 'inclusive' choice is the *selection* of a particular outcome or the desire to take a course of action. An example of 'inclusive' choice behaviour is provided by this female student from Portland School, who describes her decision-making process in Year 9.

Portland student female #3

Patrick White: So when you were in Year 9 what did you, you know, how did you make up your mind about what you were going to take?

Student: Well, some of the subjects I was absolutely certain on, like music and drama, I knew I wanted to do them. It was just a matter of seeing what subjects were grouped together and which ones I'd like to do out of the choice that I had.

Patrick White: So there wasn't a completely free choice, you couldn't just go along and choose any four?

Student: No, 'cos they were grouped together, so you couldn't do like PE and drama, because they go on at the same time, the same lesson time. So it's a matter of seeing which ones are grouped together and which ones you can do.

Patrick White: So were there any subjects that you would have taken had there been the opportunity?

Student: Yeah. I would've liked to do RE but I couldn't because I wouldn't have been able to do music.

Patrick White: Right, so they clashed?

Student: Yeah.

Patrick White: Anything else?

Student: I don't think so, I think I got most of my subjects that I wanted to do.

This extract not only illustrates the nature of an 'inclusive' choice but also demonstrates some of the restrictions faced by students at various stages of their educational careers. As will be discussed later, the nature and degree of these restrictions varied between Year 9 and Year 11 but they were often important when choosing GCSE subjects in Year 9.

In the extracts below a Year 11 student describes her decisions regarding the subjects she planned to take in the following two years. As with many students, the choice of subjects she intended to pursue was her first priority when planning her post-school destination.

Railroad female student #4

Patrick White: D'you know what you're doing next year [Year 12]?

Student: I know what I want to do next year. I want to do art and maths A-level, and theatre studies and physics AS-level.

[. . .]

Patrick White: Are these options, again, just like, you're doing what you want?

Student: Yeah. I had five. I had English, maths, art, physics, and I just decided that it wasn't a good idea for me to take English 'cause I'm not actually doing that well in English.

Patrick White: And you didn't wanna do four [A-levels]?

Student: Yeah.

Patrick White: Too much work, yeah?

Student: Yeah. But the head of the sixth form here told me that there's no point to do it anymore, because it's like, not needed. And it's too much work.

This student clearly knew what subjects she wanted to take. The 'inclusive' nature of her choice is demonstrated by her initial desire to take three subjects at A-level and a further two at AS-level. After being advised by a teacher to take fewer courses, she finally decided to take only one AS-level. Here she describes her choice of institutions:

Patrick White: D'you want to do that [art] here?

Student: Not art here. I'm doing art at the college.

Patrick White: So you can do that?

Student: Yeah.

Patrick White: I mean, could've you done art here?

Student: I could do art here, yeah.

Patrick White: And the college isn't that far?

Student: The college is just down the road. But the A-level campus, for art, is in Tackley. Which is actually good. I mean, it's a whole, it used to be a secondary school. It's, like, the whole school and they've turned it into an art school.
Patrick White: Is that why you want to go there, for the facilities?
Student: Yeah. Yeah.

Again, when choosing institutions, this student displays 'inclusive' choice behaviour regarding her choices. While continuing to study two subjects at her present institution, she also planned to attend an additional institution with specialist facilities. Splitting post-16 study over two institutions was fairly unusual behaviour among the young people interviewed. However, this student attended a school (Railroad) with strong links to the local FE college and so this kind of arrangement was more common at this institution, especially among those studying vocational subjects. Her decision to include an alternative institution in her post-16 career plans does, however, provide a clear example of an 'inclusive' choice. While choosing to be based at her school sixth form, she also intended to take advantage of resources available at a nearby specialist institution.

Two stages of this student's choice process have been illustrated, both involving 'inclusive' choices. After first making a series of choices regarding the subjects she wanted to pursue at the post-16 level, she went on to make decisions relating to post-school institutions. As was discussed earlier, her choice of subjects also involved elements of 'exclusive' decision making, and it is this type of choice that is discussed in more detail in the next section.

Exclusive choices

'Exclusive' choices, in contrast to 'inclusive' ones, start from the premise that some outcomes are to be avoided. Subsequent choices are then structured around this consideration. 'Exclusive' choices were much more common in Year 9 than in Year 11, presumably because of the restricted range of alternatives faced by students choosing their GCSE options (see later discussion). This type of choice is similar to Gorard's (1997, p. 31) 'negative choice' and has appeared as an important element in the school choice processes described by both Smedley (1995) and West and Varlaam (1991).

Bagley *et al*. (2001) argue that the 'rejection' of options is common choice behaviour among those choosing secondary schools. In relation to subject areas, Cleaves (2005, p. 482) found that students 'eliminated science from their choices by negative selection'. And in the context of further education, Aggleton (1987, p. 71), reports that 'students' curricular choices were . . . influenced by their negative evaluation of other options on offer at College.

A male student from Gordon Cole School describes the 'exclusive' nature of his decision-making process when choosing his GCSE options in Year 9.

Gordon Cole student, male #1

Patrick White: And so you'd have chosen them in Year 9 for Years 10 and 11?

Student: Yeah.

Patrick White: And how did you go about choosing those subjects?

Student: We were given like a sheet and we had to tick which ones . . . and I don't like drama and music so I got rid of those [laughs] and then pretty much I just chose the ones I knew I was doing quite well in and which I enjoyed most and I thought would probably be easy. But it's like not getting the worst: which ones not to choose and then which ones I was left with really.

[. . .]

Patrick White: So you just got rid of the ones you didn't really want to do and then saw what was left?

Student: Yeah.

Patrick White: Did you talk to your parents much about it?

Student: Yeah, yeah I did. Yeah, they didn't really have that much to say 'cos I suppose they don't really know what, yeah, I didn't talk about it that much because they knew which ones I didn't like, so [laughs].

Patrick White: So once you'd got rid of those ones it was a case of taking what was left?

Student: Yeah.

As the above extract illustrates, the student first eliminated subjects that he disliked (an 'exclusive' choice), leaving a subset of options from which to pick those he enjoyed and/or did well in. This was a fairly common course of action in Year 9, as certain subjects were compulsory and the degree of choice for other subject areas was restricted by timetabling.

More concisely expressed examples of the same process, operating at a different level, are provided by two male students, both from Portland School.

Portland student male #1

Patrick White: Oh, right. So what made you want to do the three sciences rather than the double one?

Student: Well, it was mainly 'cos if I didn't I'd have probably ended up doing history which I really didn't want to do.

Patrick White: So you're not doing history or geography?

Student: I'm just doing geography.

Patrick White: Right.

Student: It was more a case that I didn't want to do history.

This student's choice of science options is most easily understood in terms of his desire to avoid taking history. Because of the timetabling restrictions faced by small, rural schools, students were never presented with a completely free choice of 'optional' subjects. Sometimes it was the lack of flexibility in the curriculum that led students to make 'exclusive' choices.

Portland student, male #3

Patrick White: What made you choose your options at that time, was it just what interested you or did you have any sort of, you know, longer-term plans?

Student: Partly what interests me or what didn't. I certainly didn't want to do Spanish, so I had to gear it around so that I didn't do Spanish.

Again, this student engineers his Year 9 choices around the avoidance of a particular subject. In Year 11, however, 'inclusive' choices became far less common, as two factors combined to ease the restrictions on choices faced in Year 9. In Years 12 and 13 students were generally required to take far fewer subjects than they had in Years 10 and 11. For example, most students took a maximum of three A-level subjects in Years 12 and 13 (see *Railroad female student #4*) and vocational courses such as GNVQs, which often required the majority of a student's curriculum time. In addition, the range of courses and subjects on offer in these years was much greater than during compulsory schooling. These two factors resulted in choices taken in Year 11 being of a very different nature than those taken at previous educational transitions.

However, a clear example of a Year 11 student making an 'exclusive' choice is the case of the following student. He concisely summarises his position in the following line:

Gordon Cole student, male #2

Student: I don't want go to college or stay on at school, so I'm just looking around to see what I could do. But I'll probably end up doing an apprenticeship as an electrician or something like that.

It became clear over the course of the interview that, because of this student's relatively low achievement, he had been encouraged by his teachers and parents to enrol on a Modern Apprenticeship. He had no particular motivations, however, apart from the desire to leave education as soon as possible. He was willing to enter the labour market but had made no serious attempt at investigating possible areas of employment; he was merely concerned with 'excluding' himself from formal education.

The terms 'inclusive' and 'exclusive' were used well before the parallel with previous research was encountered in the literature. Other researchers, however, have documented similar phenomena. Aggleton (1987, p. 61, emphasis added) writes that 'we might therefore reasonably conclude that for many young people, the transition from school to college at 16 is motivated by both *push* and *pull* factors'. Gorard (1997) also writes about 'positive' as well as 'negative' choices relating to choosing secondary schools.

Default choices

The concept of 'default' choices was developed in response to data relating to choices made in Year 11 that could not be accommodated into the existing 'inclusive'/'exclusive' binary. 'Default' decisions, as the name suggests, are characterised by a lack of engagement by the student concerned and, perhaps, do not constitute choices or decisions in the conventional sense at all. In her review of the research on post-16 decision making, Payne (2003, pp. 8–9) notes that

> the very concept of a decision or choice may sometimes be inappropriate . . . [some young people] may act on the basis of long-standing assumptions about what they will do, probably without properly considering any alternatives.

She cites research conducted in the late 1970s to demonstrate that this phenomenon is certainly not new. Ryrie (1981, pp. 3–4, in Payne 2003, p. 11) states that

> young people come to internalise certain expectations, and adopt certain taken-for-granted assumptions . . . [which] may result in decisions being made . . . without any conscious choice on the part of the individuals.

Similarly, Hodkinson *et al.* (1996, p. 145) conclude that 'some choices . . . are not conscious, discursive choices in the way in which choice is often understood in everyday language'. Some 'default' choices certainly appear to fall into this category.

They also appear similar to what both Heath (2002) and Furlong (1992) describe as 'embedded' choices. In Heath's (2002) study of the choices of Year 11 Welsh-speaking students, she reports that some individuals' choices to continue their education through the medium of Welsh required little in the way of decision making, as it has been an assumption 'embedded' in their worldview via earlier processes of socialisation. Their ties to the language were such an integral part of their culture that the decision to change to English-medium education would not have been seriously considered, or even considered at all.

In a study in Scotland, Furlong (1992, p. 28) found that 'for many young people . . . there is no real decision to be made at the end of fourth year [Year 11 in England and Wales] about whether to stay on, as many young people had always assumed that they would start a fifth year [Year 12]'. It was fairly common for students to express similar sentiments in the present study, particularly in relation to the expectation that they would take A-levels and/or go on to study at university. They may have had parents and/or elder siblings who followed this route and had been brought up within a familial culture in which this course of action was considered to be the norm. Indeed, Furlong (1992, p. 108) writes of the important influence of 'the deeply-embedded impressions . . . developed as a result of experiences in the family and in the school'.

Another kind of behaviour that was subsumed within the 'default' category was exhibited by students who had no particular direction in mind, and made 'choices' according to the advice of others. Such behaviour was not solely associated with students who might be viewed as 'disaffected' or in some way dissatisfied with the education system, but all the students concerned appeared to suffer from a lack of engagement with the post-16 decision-making process. Only very few students fell into this category and the common theme of 'inaction' meant that they were also coded as making 'default' choices. In a larger-scale study, with a greater number and variety of such cases, it may have been possible to conceptualise such behaviour differently. However, given its relative scarcity in the present study, this was not possible.

Furlong (2005, p. 385) noted behaviour of a similar kind amongst a 'sizable group' of young people. He reports that

> Among those who stayed on due to an absence of attractive alternatives in the labour market are a sizable group of young people who drifted through the upper secondary school, collecting some additional qualifications without having any developed idea about where continued study may be leading them in career terms: these young people are able to avoid decisions about their educational futures until age 18.

'Default' decisions are difficult to illustrate using short interview extracts as, by definition, they are often characterised by *inaction*. Unsurprisingly, some students tended to be reticent about admitting that they had withdrawn from, or never actively engaged with, the decision-making process. 'Default' choices were often couched in either 'inclusive' or 'exclusive' terms before the actual nature of the decision became clear. This is illustrated below in an extract from an interview with a male student at Kingfisher School:

Kingfisher student, male, #6

Patrick White: Have you ever thought of going to some college somewhere?
Student: I haven't really thought about it, no.
Patrick White: Is it sort of a natural thing to stay on?
Student: Yeah.
[. . .]
Patrick White: You reckon that if you get the grades you'll be staying on here?
Student: Yeah, I would have thought so. Unless a decent job comes along.
Patrick White: Have you been, like, looking for any jobs? Or are you just going to see what happens?
Student: See what happens really. I've got a summer job which I can work at, I expect. It's alright for now.
[. . .]
Patrick White: But do you reckon your mum would rather you stay on than get a job?
Student: Well, I don't know. Staying on seems like a good idea, but . . .
Patrick White: So, what subjects would you want to be taking?
Student: I haven't really thought about that.

In the above extract the student explains that he will probably continue with his studies at his present institution (an 11 to 18 comprehensive school). He has no particularly strong desires to pursue particular subjects or qualifications and even suggests that he may take up employment if 'a decent job comes along'.

This example perhaps demonstrates a negative side of 'default' choice that was relatively uncommon amongst the students interviewed. For a few students, staying in education represented an opportunity to avoid engaging with the choices they are faced with at the end of Year 11. Indeed, this is exactly the kind of motive that was reported by Furlong (2005). Continuing study to the post-16 level is a course of action that is rarely questioned (as leaving school for work might) as it constitutes the route taken by the majority of young people at this stage of their careers. However, as the case above demonstrates, it is not always the result of an active decision-making behaviour but rather the consequence of avoiding the choices which are faced at this point of transition.

'Default' decisions can, however, be much more neutral. The example below illustrates a tendency of some students, based in 11–18 schools, not to consider seriously the possibility of moving institutions.

Portland student male #1

Patrick White: You say they want you to stay on at Portland, have you seriously considered going anywhere else?

Student: No. It might be because they've [student's parents] said they want me to stay on, but I've not thought about it at all.

Patrick White: Are any of your friends leaving to go to other places?

Student: No. I think there are a few going but mainly that's because they don't do the subjects here.

Another common example of a 'default' choice was the decision to pursue A-level qualifications with the assumption that a university place would follow. The following extract provides an example of this phenomenon.

Portland student female #5

Patrick White: Have you thought about what you want to do after the sixth form?

Student: Well, I thought I would just get my A-levels and go to university somewhere, get a degree if they'll let me in!

Patrick White: Right. Is that what your parents expect of you or is it something you'd do anyway?

Student: It's something I'd do anyway. I've been going to do that all my life anyway, when I've finished school to go to university. They expect me to do that anyway.

The above extract, although brief, illustrates a number of phenomena. First, the student concerned had firm plans to enter the higher education sector while still in Year 11. More interestingly, however, is the revelation that she had 'been going to do that all my [her] life' and the indication of a similar long-term parental expectation. Such decisions to stay in education and to take A-levels are similar to the kind of 'embedded' choices described by Heath (2002) and Furlong (1992) and can therefore be conceptualised as 'default' choice behaviour.

Primary, secondary and tertiary choice stages

In addition to differentiating between different 'types' of decision making engaged in by students, it was evident that students made more than one decision at each transition. Although, for reasons already discussed, it was often to separate decision regarding subjects, qualifications and institutions, where possible students' choices were divided into different stages. These 'stages' are briefly discussed below, before they are integrated with the choice 'types' to form models of decision-making behaviour (see Figures 4.2 and 4.4, that appear later).

The 'primary' stage

There are problems both with determining the sequence of the different choice 'stages' and their relative importance to students but the 'primary' stage generally represented the first stage of the students' decision-making process. As the initial stage of the choice process, the 'primary' stage was engaged with by all students in Years 9 and 11.

It was common, but not inevitable, for students to act according to their first priorities at this stage of the choice process. For example, a Year 9 student may have a strong desire (for whatever reason) to take three science GCSEs. Their 'primary' choice (in this case an 'inclusive' one) would be, therefore, to take these three subjects. In any subsequent stage of the choice process in that year they would pick other options to fit around this choice. Another example might be a student who wished to avoid a particular subject or teacher. Their 'primary' choice (in this case an 'exclusive' one) would involve taking a subject combination which ensured that the subject or teacher in question would not be included in their Key Stage 4 timetable.

It is important, however, not to confuse choice 'types' and 'stage' with the rationales and motives that underlie them. For example, the desire to pursue a career as a veterinarian is not, in itself, a 'primary choice'. It may, however, set an agenda to which decisions must comply, including the need to take two or three science subjects at GCSE.

The 'secondary' and 'tertiary' stages

Although the choice models in both Year 9 and Year 11 include 'primary' and 'secondary' choice stages, only the Year 11 model has a 'tertiary' stage. There are a variety of reasons for this relating to, first, the diversity of individuals' choice processes and, second, the differences in the nature of the choices to be made in the two years.

As students progress through their educational career, the choices they face become increasing complex. Year 11 choices involve a consideration not only of which subjects to take but also decisions regarding both qualifications and institutions, and thus are more likely to comprise more than one choice 'stage'. The students' accounts reflected this and the final version of the choice model developed to describe decision making in that year was considerably more complex than that for Year 9 (see later discussion).

An example from the data

As with default choices, it is difficult to adequately illustrate choice stages with short extracts from the interviews. Both phenomena can be seen more clearly through an examination of complete narratives. To facilitate this, complete transcripts of the student interviews, in pseudonomised form, were attached electronically as text files on a CD-ROM appendix to the original report (White 2002).

However, to allow an insight into the analytic process, extracts from one interview are included here, accompanied by an explanation of the logic used in the analysis.

Meadow Lane student female #2

Patrick White: [. . .] So what are you planning to do next year?

Student: English literature, history and biology. I'm undecided about a third . . . [and] a fourth . . . I might either do a fourth A-level or an AS. I'm definitely going to have three and a half.

Patrick White: In what?

Student: I'm not really sure yet, it's either going to be in music, religious studies or chemistry, or possibly psychology.

[. . .]

Patrick White: Okay. So you want to do English literature, history and what was the other one?

Student: Biology.

Patrick White: Biology and, that's kind of an odd mix, and another maybe half or full?

Student: Well, I think biology is a bit, but I think I was also going to do religious studies, I think the three would go really well, but I figured there might be too much essay writing. Also I thought the universities might look for somebody who's sort of got another aspect. I don't know, just something more. I don't really know what they're expecting, so . . .

Patrick White: Have you been, has there been anything at school about university requirements?

Student: No, not really. I did the graduate opportunities course last year and we went along and saw Bath University, found out a bit about it, had a lecture on business studies which put me off doing business studies totally unfortunately [laughs].

Patrick White: Was that something you were considering then, or . . .?

Student: Not seriously, but I hadn't thought 'I'm definitely not going to do that!' and now it's like, 'No way, I would not do it' (laughs). But it was nice seeing round the university and see all the different colleges and we found out that, you know, you have to have a GCSE grade B in maths and we hadn't been told that before.

Patrick White: To do what?

Student: To be accepted into that university.
[. . .]
Patrick White: Do you want to go to Davchester College?
Student: I would like to, I'm not sure if I'm going to or not. Looking at Chalfont College, Chalfont Boys' College. 'Cause they're going co-ed next year.
Patrick White: What are your parents' thoughts about that?
Student: They would rather I went there than Davchester College. They think I need a change and a stronger structure.
Patrick White: Is that a fee-paying school or . . .?
Student: Yes.
Patrick White: Right.
Student: I mean I'm not into that sort of thing. I mean, I think it's good if you've sort of been into the system all your life but as you change I think it's really, really difficult and it's quite a big jump. I'm not sure. But if I went there it'd be boarding . . .
Patrick White: Oh, right
Student: Which would be quite cool.
Patrick White: What after last time?
Student: Yes.

The extracts above are presented in the order they arose in the interview. In the first extract, when the student is asked about her intentions for Year 12, she frames her answer in terms of subjects and qualifications. Unprompted, she talks about university entrance in the second extract and in the third she discusses post-16 institutions. The second extract suggests that entering university is her main priority and that she has already thought about academic entry requirements. Although she is undecided about what course she might pursue in higher education, she is concerned about the implication of her subject combinations at A-level for university entrance.

Considering the above, this student's choices were divided into the following choice stages. The choice to take A-levels was coded as her 'primary' choice, given her over-riding concerns about entering university. At no point in the interview were other qualifications (apart from additional AS-levels) were discussed as potential alternatives. As she had assumed she would be going to university since an early age, her primary choice was categorised as a 'default' one.

As she was undecided about what course she would prefer to study in higher education, and was primarily concerned about a subject combination which would maximise her opportunities in terms of university entrance, her choice of A-level *subjects* was coded as the 'secondary' choice stage. That she was still unsure about which post-16 institutions she would apply to suggests that this decision has not yet been resolved and so this was coded as the 'tertiary' choice stage. Although it is also the case that she had not finalised her choice of post-16 subjects, she was fairly certain about three subjects and this choice appeared to be nearer to completion than decisions regarding institutions.

It is accepted that it is not possible to ascertain whether these stages are either artefacts of the focus of the research, the interview situation, the ability of students to recall past events or conversational conventions. They are used here more as an heuristic device than a definitive conclusion about the order in which students make choices, or the relative importance each choice stage assumes. The separation of these stages sometimes reflects the *order* in which the choices arose but on other occasions do not. Decisions regarding the boundaries and order of stages were only made after a thorough examination of each interview transcript and a consideration of each young person's account.

Choice models

It is now possible to demonstrate how these categories fit into the choice models that were constructed. These models are described in terms of their historical development over the course of the analysis. The discussion also provides further insight into the development of the choice 'types' and 'stages' described above, and illustrates the iterative nature of the analysis. The choice models are presented in the chronological order in which they were developed, and the processes of their modification and adaptation are described in full.

Choice in Year 9

In Year 9 students were faced with a choice of optional subjects to complement those that were mandatory. During the analysis of the data relating to choices at this transition, choice behaviour could be unproblematically categorised as either 'inclusive' or 'exclusive'. There was, at this point in the analysis, no need to create the 'default' category that was necessary to conceptualise decision-making behaviour in Year 11.

That a simpler choice typology provided an adequate conceptualisation of Year 9 decision making may be a result of the restricted nature of the choices faced at that time. 'Option' subjects had to be chosen from a limited selection and timetabling often dictated the scope of choice available. As *Portland student female #3* stated, 'It was just a matter of seeing what subjects were grouped together and which ones I'd like to do out of the choice that I had.'

However, it is also possible that the typology was an artefact of the students' accounts, reconstructed from memories of events that took place two years before they were interviewed. As was explained in Chapter 3, choices in Year 9 were not originally intended to be examined but were included only after students repeatedly raised their connection with choices in Year 11. And as data relating to decision making in Year 9 are substantially weaker than students' accounts of choices behaviour in Year 11, this should be taken into account when assessing the validity and utility of the models. This is not to say, however, that the Year 9 choice model is of no value, only that its origins in the data should be considered if it is to be generalised beyond the data from which it originated.

The first version of the Year 9 choice model was a matrix comprising of one row and two columns, and is shown in Figure 4.1. This model was based on the preliminary stages of analysis, described above. At this stage of the analysis the idea of choice stages had not been fully explored and the concepts of 'inclusive' and 'exclusive' decisions satisfactorily differentiated between the two main approaches to the choice process identified in the students' accounts. However, when this model was tested rigorously against all the cases in the sample, it was apparent that it did not adequately

	Type of Choice: Inclusive	Exclusive
GCSE Subject Choice	A	B

Figure 4.1 Choice in Year 9 (GCSE options) – version 1.

Choice Order:	Type of Choice:	
	Inclusive	Exclusive
Primary	A	B
Secondary	C	D

Figure 4.2 Choices in Year – version 2.

describe the choice processes of a significant minority of students (n = 13). These individuals, once having made an 'inclusive' or 'exclusive' choice, then went on to make a further choice, which could be of either type. It was then that the idea of 'choice stages' was employed for the first time. The decision making process was broken down into two such 'stages', leading to a second version of the model (Figure 4.2).

This second model was deemed satisfactory in its ability to capture the nature of the choice process in Year 9 as it appeared in the students' narratives. Its constituent concepts also served as a starting point for the analysis of the data relating to Year 11 decision making.

Choice in Year 11

For a number of related reasons, decisions in Year 11 were much more complex than those faced in Year 9. First, as has already been noted, in Year 11 young people were only required to choose a small number of courses (usually between one and three) from a vast array of available alternatives. Indeed, Bell *et al.* (2005), in a review of patterns uptake on post-16 qualifications, comment on the 'sheer number of different combinations of A-levels taken'. Additionally, students were required to make decisions not only about the subject areas they wished to pursue but also about qualification types and institutions. This resulted in a huge increase in the number of options they faced.

Choices relating to post-16 destinations were particularly different to Year 9 choices because of a relative lack of restrictions placed on the particular direction an individual wished to follow. Students were neither compelled to remain in school nor the education system as a whole, and there were no nationally regulated subject combinations or specific subjects that were compulsory at that level. Second, as

Choice Order:	Type of Choice: Inclusive	Exclusive	Default
Primary	A	C	E
Secondary	B	D	F

Figure 4.3 Year 11 choice model – version 1.

their labour market and/or higher education careers are much closer than in Year 9, decisions in Year 11 were more likely to have direct implications for routes to these destinations.

The differences in the choices faced by students in Years 9 and 11 impacted on their choice behaviour at these two transition points and meant that the Year 11 choices could not be adequately contained within the choice model developed for Year 9. While the Year 9 model and its constituent concepts were used as the 'building blocks' for the Year 11 model, it required modification in order to accommodate the greater scope for choice in the latter year.

This first, and most significant change was the addition of a further choice 'type', later labelled 'default' (see previous discussion), needed to encompass the full range of choice behaviour described by the students. This was added to the existing choice types and incorporated into the vertical axis of the model (Figure 4.3).

However, this was not the only change that was required. Because of the multifaceted nature of choices in Year 11, some students engaged in more than two choice 'stages' before coming to a final decision and so, in a similar manner to the modifications of the Year 9 model, an additional 'stage' needed to be added. The final choice model for the Year 11 decision-making process is shown in Figure 4.4.

Students' decision making in both Year 9 and Year 11 can be usefully understood as comprising action operating along two axes: choice types and choice stages. This model inevitably represents a simplified approximation of students' choice behaviour and strictly speaking represents their accounts of the decision making process rather than the process as it took place. However, at the very least it provides insight into students' constructions of their decision making.

Choice Stage:	Type of Choice: Inclusive	Exclusive	Default
Primary	A	D	G
Secondary	B	E	H
Tertiary	C	F	I

Figure 4.4 Year 11 choice model – version 2.

The extent to which this accurately reflects their choice behaviour can only be revealed through further study.

The distribution of choice behaviour

Before moving on to the motivations that were behind the young people's decision-making behaviour, the issue of the extent to which the two choice models represent the student sample is addressed. As discussed in Chapter 2, numeric summaries are used throughout this book in order to illustrate the characteristics and behaviour of the entire student sample. This reduces the likelihood of the findings being viewed as merely anecdotal, and provides a context within which interview extracts can be located.

Choice in Year 9

The majority (41/54) of students were able to complete the Year 9 decision-making process after only one choice 'stage'. This may best be explained by the relatively restricted nature of Year 9 choices, as compulsory subjects limit the degree of flexibility in the Year 10 and Year 11 curriculum. As the range of real choice relating to option subjects is often very limited, the decision-making process is simplified correspondingly.

Figure 4.5 shows the number and types of choice made at the different choice stages. However, a number of points must be made before the data can be properly interpreted. First, five of the students' choices were not included in this model, as they had little memory of the Year 9 choice process, meaning that only 54 of 59 students could

Choice Stage:	Type of Choice: Inclusive	Exclusive	Total
Primary	49	5	54
Secondary	5	16	21 **
Total number of choices	54	21	75

Figure 4.5 Year 9 choice frequencies.
* All 54 students necessarily engaged with the primary choice stage.
** 33 out of 54 students completed the choice process in the 'primary' stage.

be included in this analysis. Second, only 21 students made choices at both the 'primary' and 'secondary' stages. The total number of choices includes the 33 single choices of the 33 students who used only the primary choice stage and the 42 choices of the 21 students who required both 'primary' and 'secondary' stages to complete the choice process.

As can be seen, the choices made in Year 9 were overwhelmingly 'inclusive' in nature. This was primarily the result of students choosing subjects they performed well in or enjoyed (see Chapter 5). There are, however, a significant minority of exclusive choices, particularly at the 'secondary' choice stage. Students who had initially chosen their preferred subjects were sometimes left with additional decisions to make and so resorted to 'excluding' their least favourite subjects (or teachers). It appears to be the case that while the majority of students resolved their decision-making process with one (usually 'inclusive') choice, the minority who went on to make further decisions were most likely to make an 'exclusive' choice at the 'secondary' stage.

Choice routes in Year 11

The phenomenon of students resorting to 'exclusive' decisions when faced with restricted choices was particularly evident in Year 9. Although there was evidence of similar behaviour in relation to decision making in Year 11, the wider range of options available meant that it was not so pronounced and the overwhelming majority of choices made at all three choice stages in Year 11 were 'inclusive' in

Choice Stage:	Type of Choice:			Totals
	Inclusive	Exclusive	Default	
Primary	50	2	7	59
Secondary	49	2	8	59
Tertiary	37	0	17	54*
Totals	136	4	32	172

Figure 4.6 Year 11 choice, by 'type' and 'stage'.

* Five students completed their decision making by the end of the secondary stage.

nature. Out of a total of 172 choices, only four 'exclusive' ones were made; two each at the 'primary' and 'secondary' stages. 'Default' choices, making up just under one-fifth (32/172) of all decisions, increased in each successive stage (7/59, 8/59, 17/54). In contrast, inclusive ones declined (50/59, 49/59, 37/54) both absolutely and proportionately.

The 'exclusive' choices that were evident in Year 9 almost disappear in Year 11 (see Figure 4.6) and, as previously noted, may be linked to the restricted set of available options that compelled students to avoid undesirable outcomes. 'Inclusive' choices, in contrast, were popular in Year 11, when students were faced with a wide range of opportunities.

The relatively high number of 'inclusive' and 'exclusive' choices in both years point to a group of young people actively engaged in decision making. As both types of choices are necessarily active, whereas 'default' choices may be considered to be more passive in nature, the evidence suggests that students were on the whole involved in, rather than detached from, the decision-making process in Year 11.

It is important to note, however, that the numeric summary provided in Figure 4.6 over-represents individuals who engaged in three choice stages at the expense of the five students who characterised their decision making in terms of only two stages. This is particularly important given the reliance of the research on students' accounts of their behaviour, rather than the behaviour itself, and raises a related issue. It is clearly plausible that young people with higher levels of literacy and oral skills were able to articulate their decision making more clearly, and consequently their accounts were much easier to separate into three distinct stages. It is possible that similar decision-making processes may have been undertaken by the five students who appeared to have finalised their choices after only two stages, the only difference being between the nature of the narratives provided during the interviews.

Given these concerns, the data relating to choice types provided in Figures 4.5 and 4.6 should only be used as an approximate indicator of their distribution amongst the sample. It serves primarily to show the relative importance of different types of choice behaviour, presented as aggregates, in the two different years.

Summary

Bearing in mind the caveats that have been highlighted throughout this chapter, some interesting patterns were discovered in relation to Year 9 and Year 11. 'Exclusive' choices, most prevalent in Year 9, may be associated with a restricted set of available options that compel students to avoid undesirable outcomes. 'Inclusive' choices, in contrast, were most popular in Year 11, when students are faced by the wide range of opportunities open to them at the post-16 level.

The relatively high number of 'inclusive' and 'exclusive' choices in both years, however, point to a group of young people actively engaged in decision making. As both types of choice are necessarily 'active', whereas 'default' choices are less clearly so, students on the whole appear to be involved in, rather than detached from, the decision-making process.

The way in which students make choices is only one dimension of decision making. Investigating the motives behind their decisions is vital to a comprehensive understanding of choice behaviour. Chapter 5 examines the motivations underlying the choices students made in Year 9, while Chapter 6 develops a more sophisticated typology of Year 11 choice motivations.

5 Choice Motivations in Year 9

Introduction

The previous chapter documented the attempt to create a 'model' of decision making using the constituent choice 'types' and 'stages' that emerged during the analysis of the student interviews. Chapters 5 and 6 examine the reasons students gave when asked why they were taking a particular course of action. Because the nature of the students' accounts and the choices they faced were different in the two transitions that were studied, the analytic categories that were used are different in both years. Whilst in Year 11 the analysis is divided into an examination of 'factors' and 'rationales', the analysis of Year 9 choices is uni-dimensional.

As discussed in Chapter 4, the choice process in Year 9 is relatively hermetic, contained as it is within the context of the secondary school curriculum and confined to decisions relating only to subject choice. Although students had chosen their GCSE options less than two years before their interviews, a minority (n = 9) either were not able to describe their experience of the Year 9 choice process at all or could not explain it in sufficient detail for their rationales and motivations to be categorised.

While some students provided only one reason for the decisions they made in Year 9, the majority (33/49) provided two completely separate rationales for their choices. After the categories used to describe the different types of motivation are discussed, their distribution among the student sample is examined.

Motivation types

When coding the data relating to Year 9 choices, it was necessary to satisfy two potentially opposing criteria: to reduce the diversity of responses into a manageable number of categories whilst ensuring that as little meaning as possible was lost in this process. In all, five categories were used to summarise the different motivations expressed by the students: enjoyment; perceptions of their own abilities and/or performance; utility; vocational aspirations and the avoidance of subjects and/or teachers. Each of these is discussed separately, below.

Enjoyment

The most common motivation given by students for their decisions in Year 9 was that previous experience had shown certain subjects to be more enjoyable than others. Such 'inclusive' rationales were based on an individual's intrinsic interest in the subject(s), and their preference for teachers and/or particular teaching methods. In contrast, some students engaging in 'exclusive' choice behaviour chose to avoid particular subjects precisely because they *did not* enjoy certain elements connected with studying them. However, both motivations relate to the degree to which a particular subject was enjoyed.

A distinguishing feature of this particular category appears to be gratification in the near or immediate future. Many students who were undecided on particular career directions in Year 9 reported taking the subjects they enjoyed most. The two students below talk about choosing their Year 9 GCSE options in this way:

Gordon Cole student male #4
Partick White: How did you go about choosing those options in Year 9?
Student: I chose the ones first I found interesting.

Gordon Cole student female #2
Partick White: And if you think back to Year 9 what went on when you were supposed to choose them?
Student: I think we were told to take the ones that we really liked . . . and I particularly wanted to take drama . . . I can't remember anything else.

These extracts are fairly typical of responses in this category. The students recount their choices in terms of the subjects they 'found interesting' or 'really liked'. In the second extract the student even suggests that this was exactly what they were instructed to do, presumably by careers or subject teachers. The two extracts below demonstrated slightly different, but related, phenomenon:

Railroad student female #4

Partick White: You didn't talk to your parents about it [choosing Year 9 options]?

Student: Oh, yeah. Yeah, I would've. But, I mean, that [combination of subjects] was what I wanted to do. So . . .

Partick White: Is that just because you wanted to take the subjects?

Student: Yeah.

Partick White: Not related to what you want to do eventually?

Student: No.

Kingfisher student male #7

Partick White: So, when you took your subjects in Year 9 and took your options for Years 10 and 11, did you have that at the back of your mind . . . that you might need certain subjects . . .?

Student: It was in the back of my mind but . . . I just chose the subjects I enjoy really.

These two students, even when asked directly, did not recall considering their future intentions or plans when choosing their Year 9 options. They re-affirmed that they were thinking, at that time, mainly in terms of the immediate consequences of the decisions they were about to make. Some did confess, however, that with the benefit of hindsight their past choices now appeared more important than they had done at the time they were made.

The four examples already presented show the interaction of 'inclusive' choice behaviour with rationales based around 'enjoyment'. Some choices exemplified the same motivation to 'exclude' certain subjects:

Portland student male #1

Patrick White: Oh, right. So what made you want to do the three sciences rather than the double one?

Student: Well, it was mainly 'cos if I didn't I'd have probably ended up doing history which I really didn't want to do.
Patrick White: So you're not doing history or geography?
Student: I'm just doing geography.
Patrick White: Right.
Student: It was more a case that I didn't want to do history.
Patrick White: But the sciences are okay then?
Student: Yes.
Patrick White: You weren't particularly passionate about them?
Student: No . . . [laughs]

This student expressed his desire to 'exclude' certain subjects that he did not want to take. Although he does not explicitly mention enjoyment, it is implicit in his narrative. It is interesting that the limited range of choice available in Year 9 often led to students making choices in terms of 'damage limitation'; they were willing to accept *less* desirable options in order to avoid the *least* desirable ones.

Railroad student female #5, below, also demonstrates an element of 'exclusive' decision making. It is interesting, however, that it is difficult to separate her enjoyment of a subject with her performance in it. She initially reports that she 'was told [she] was good at drama' before going on to justify her choice in terms of enjoyment.

Railroad student female #5
Patrick White: Right. So, if you can remember that far back, when you were, when you made these decisions on what to take, I mean, how did you make them?
Student: . . . [no response]
Patrick White: Did you do the things you liked? Did you talk to your mum about them? What, sort of, made you decide?
Student: Well I got told I was good at drama. So I said to my mum, 'Well I want to do drama 'cause I like it and enjoy it'. So she said, 'Well do drama'. And I done DOVE [Diploma of Vocational Education] 'cause I didn't wanna do art [laughs]. And I didn't wanna do PE either [laughs]. And it was something different as well.

Patrick White: Right. So, I mean, did you . . . so it was a case of, sort of, which one's you didn't want to do and which ones were left then at the end of it?
Student: Well, yeah.

Unsurprisingly, it was common for students to report enjoying the subjects in which they performed well. However, this is potentially problematic for the taxonomy of motivations provided here and may weaken their explanatory power. Nevertheless, because many students made a clear distinction between the two rationales, these were kept as separate categories, whilst acknowledging this potential limitation. The importance of students' performance in subjects in relation to their decision making is explored next.

Performance

Students' perceptions of their ability in particular subjects also influenced their decisions in Year 9. Unsurprisingly, students were more likely to take subjects in which they were confident about their ability. This was often discussed in conjunction with statements concerned with 'enjoyment' but, interestingly, 'ability' was *only* mentioned by students who gave more than one reason for their choice. As discussed previously, it may be that 'ability' and 'enjoyment' are not analytically separable but closely related phenomenon. The following extract provides an example of this kind of reasoning.

Railroad student male #5
Student: I chose the ones that I wanted to do and which I found easy. Not 'easy' easy, but what I felt I could be comfortable with.

Railroad student male #5 demonstrates the kind of connection that some students made between their ability in a subject (or how 'easy' they found it) and their immediate feelings of security (or 'comfort'). He also describes choosing subjects he 'wanted to do', but it is less clear about exactly *why* he wanted to do them. Whether there were additional criteria involved in his choice process, or whether he only wished to take those subjects he excelled in, is unclear from his account. The student in the next extract makes a similar connection between those subjects she was 'best at' and those that she enjoyed.

Meadow Lane student female #4

Patrick White: In Year 9 when you took your options, how did you go about deciding which subjects you wanted to take?

Student: We had an options evening, and there was lots of information about the courses, and that helped me a bit, and what I chose was those that I thought I'd be best at, the ones I enjoy.

Again, it is not clear from this extract how closely the criteria of 'enjoyment' and 'ability' are linked, conceptually, for these students. Neither account provides a clear distinction between the two factors. In the extract below, however, the student makes an explicit link between his 'enjoyment' of a subject and his performance.

Meadow Lane student male #2

Patrick White: So when you were taking your options in Year 9, what sort of, how did you go about choosing the ones you took?

Student: Erm . . . I mainly chose the ones I like doing, 'cos I usually find that if I like doing it I'm better at it, 'cos if don't [like doing it] I just get bored.

Here a positive connection is made between enjoyment of a subject and performance in it. Examples can also be found in which students express their belief in the same phenomenon, acting in the opposite direction (i.e. disliking subjects in which they did not perform well and so avoiding them). Indeed, a link between 'ability' and 'enjoyment' appeals to a commonsense logic. However, because of the limited size of this sub-sample, and the small number of students making such connections, there was insufficient data to explore this relationship further.

It is clear from the analysis that the way in which some students perceive their ability and subsequent performance in certain subjects can affect their choices in Year 9. The extracts show various ways in which this link is expressed by the students themselves, but it is not clear to what extent, or for whom, 'ability' is separable from 'enjoyment'. 'Ability' was not used by any students in this sub-sample as the *sole* rationale for their choices and students rarely made any explicit reference to their future exam performance when discussing Year 9 choices (although they may *implicitly* assume that this is an assumption shared by the interviewer). As is discussed later in this chapter, the two motives often appear side-by-side in students' accounts. However, this is not always the case and 'enjoyment' often appears as a separate consideration.

Vocational goals

A number of students (n = 14) reported making choices for reasons relating to long-term goals. These motivations were categorised as 'vocational'. They related not only to specific (or more general) occupational aspirations but also to plans regarding FE or HE destinations. During the first stages of the analysis, motivations relating to FE, HE, training and the labour market were separated into separate groups. However, because there was often considerable overlap between these groups (e.g. a student needing to go on to *both* FE and HE in order to eventually become a veterinarian), and because of the relatively small number of students referring to these concerns (14/48), the sub-groups were collapsed into a single, larger category.

The three extracts below illustrate some of the ways in which Year 9 choices could be influenced by students' intentions regarding further and higher education.

Railroad student female #3

Patrick White: So what made you choose the subjects that you took? You choose those in Year 9, yeah?

Student: Year 10.

Patrick White: But you make the choice the year before?

Student: Yeah. If I can remember rightly, yeah. I chose art because I know that I wanted to go into an art course. And I think I'm quite good at art and I reckon I can push myself to do a lot better. PE [physical education] I like doing anyway, I'm very active some teachers say [laughs].

Portland student female #3

Student: Yeah, the teachers who were organising it, they told us to talk to our parents about it and not to rush the decisions that we made. And so I sort of sat down with my mum, we talked about what subjects would be useful to me when I go on to, sort of, to college and things, what subjects I might need for the courses I wanted to do, that I'm thinking about.

Patrick White: So at that time what did you have in mind about what you wanted to do?

Student: Well, I wanted to be a teacher, of possibly music and drama, so I needed to do double science because it's sort of a wider range of science than single, and I needed to do obviously music and drama [laughs]. But maths and English were ones that were compulsory anyway.

Railroad student male #1

Patrick White: I see. So, I mean, did you ever think, when you were in Year 9, about what you were going to do after sixteen, I mean . . .?

Student: Er, yeah. I've always wanted to, er, go to university.

Patrick White: Right. Did you have any idea about what you wanted to do, or did you just, sort of, want to go to university?

Student: Well, sort of, I don't know, but, I keep changing that. I wanted to be a doctor in Year 9, but don't now.

Patrick White: Right. Did that influence your choosing the triple science at the time?

Student: It did, yeah. Because I thought that'd help.

All these students made choices that would facilitate their post-16 intentions, as they perceived them in Year 9. The first student took an art GCSE because she planned to continue studying the subject after leaving compulsory schooling. She also reports that her ability in this subject was a factor in her choice. Here is an example of 'performance' not only affecting immediate choices of GCSE options but influencing a longer-term trajectory. It is interesting, however, that while this student mentions 'enjoyment' as a consideration, this is not specifically directed towards her choosing art, the subject she wishes to continue with post-16, but a different GCSE option (PE).

The second student considers both FE (and perhaps also HE – the term 'college' is ambiguous) and a particular vocational direction when deciding on her choices. Neither of these considerations were commonly reported by students as important to them in Year 9. Indeed, it was noticeable that most students made no reference to *any* events taking place after Year 10. The fact that participation in some form of further education or training was the norm for over three-quarters of 16–18 year-olds for the three years these students had been in secondary education (see Chapter 2) makes it particularly surprising that they do not report considering their post-16 futures whilst in Year 9.

The third student's choices were also influenced by two considerations; the idea of continuing into higher education and the ambition to become a doctor (the latter abandoned by Year 11). His occupational plans were most influential in deciding his GCSE choices, as the entry route to the profession requires a more specific set of qualifications than does entry to HE *per se*. However, along with the other two cases, he represents a small minority of students who reported thinking about post-16 education or training while making decisions in Year 9.

Given Taylor's (1992) finding that few students had firm occupational aspirations even by Year 11, it is not particularly surprising that very few students were motivated by such factors when choosing their GCSE options in Year 9. However, it was anticipated that a greater proportion would have considered possible post-16 destinations at this point. 'Vocational' motivations included those relating to future plans regarding education and training but less than one-third of the sample (14/48) mentioned *either* occupation, education, *or* training-related reasons for the choices they made in Year 9. A much larger number reported the desire to keep their post-16 options 'open' but such responses were categorised as relating to the 'utility' of the subjects in a broader sense than any particular career plans. As no student mentioned both 'vocational' and 'utility' motivations this was not problematic in terms of the analysis.

There was a contrast between the majority of students, who were not thinking beyond their immediate educational futures, and a small minority, who chose their GCSE subjects with occupational destinations, or at least further and higher education, in mind. It would be unrealistic to expect all Year 9 students to have decided on a specific area of employment which they would like to enter while still two years from the completion of compulsory schooling. But given contemporary trends in post-16 participation, the fact that only a few students reported having given any thought to their post-16 options when choosing their GCSEs was somewhat surprising.

Utility

In contrast to the 'vocational' rationales discussed above, those categorised under the heading of 'utility' relate to students' concerns about the value of particular subjects in quite general terms, rather than in terms of a particular vocational or educational pathway. Several students expressed their desire to keep their 'options open' whilst others provided more detailed explanations. The young person below talks about deciding how many science modules to take, a choice faced by nearly all Year 9 students.

Portland student female #3

Patrick White: So you've decided to do double science. Why did you decide to do double science?

Student: Well if you do single science you can't go on to do any science for an A-level, so it's just sort of a safer option to take double, in case I change my mind about something and decided I want to go on to something else.

Patrick White: So at the time you weren't thinking of doing science things, but you thought you better do it just in case?

Student: It'd be safer to do it.

The student explains her decision to take two science subjects in terms of it representing a 'safer' option than taking only a single science GCSE. Schools generally offer between one and three science modules at this level but do not all offer a single science option. Most students in the sample chose to take 'double science' and were generally encouraged to do so by teachers. As the student above explains, these decisions could have direct implications for possible routes at the end of compulsory schooling (see also Cleaves 2005). Indeed, several students referred to this kind of motive in more general terms, believing the choice of a broad range of subjects would help achieve this goal.

It is important to note at this stage that among the few students who had firm vocational ambitions when interviewed in Year 11, even fewer had the same goals two years beforehand. As already discussed, it was fairly unusual for students to consider specific occupational requirements when making decisions in Year 9. In fact, students were as likely to engage in the kind of behaviour seen in the extracts directly above, where vocational decisions were deferred and GCSE subjects were chosen with the aim of keeping as many avenues open as possible. However, this type of pragmatic, strategic behaviour was still relatively uncommon. As stated earlier, most individuals reported having chosen their GCSE options without giving a great deal of thought to their educational or occupational futures.

With respect to judging the relative 'utility' of different subjects, it was not always clear where the students obtained the information needed to make their choices. Many mentioned discussions with their parents and with subject teachers. The nature of the information provided by these different sources is likely to differ, which could help explain the characteristics of some of the rationales provided.

Students like *Portland student female #3*, who considered the implications of their GCSE choices for routes into further and higher education, represent one type of chooser, with a particular interpretation of 'utility'. The extracts below are from interviews with two students, one male and one female, both attending different schools, who describe a slightly different conception of 'utility' to the one just discussed.

Kingfisher student male #9

Patrick White: And you chose those in Year 9, yes?

Student: Yes.

Patrick White: And how did you choose them? Was it just the stuff that you liked?

Student: Yes . . . yes . . . and stuff that I thought would be interesting and useful . . . because I was going to do drama . . . and I thought those [geography, business studies and information technology (IT)] were probably worth more in the long run.

Patrick White: What, in terms of getting a job?

Student: Yes, in terms of getting a job.

Gordon Cole student female #1

Patrick White: Right. And why did you choose them?

Student: Er . . . I chose to do IT . . . I thought it would help in the future. I wish I hadn't taken it now, it's

awful. Business studies 'cos it sounded all right and 'cos it helps a lot.
Patrick White: Helps in what way?
Student: In any way.

In the first of these extracts (*Kingfisher student male #9*) the student contrasts his initial thoughts with his final decision. He eventually decided against taking drama as he believed that the other subjects he had considered (geography, business studies and IT) would 'probably [be] worth more in the long run'. Although he justifies this in relation to job prospects, this is only after the suggestion is made by the interviewer. The second extract demonstrates a similar rationale. Again, IT is seen as a subject which 'would help in the future'. As in the first extract business studies is mentioned, however when pressed on the subject, the student is unclear exactly how it would be useful.

It is certainly the case that several students who gave accounts similar to these reported discussions with their parents regarding the advantages and disadvantages of different subjects. The two examples above appear to reflect views based on commonplace assumptions and 'folk knowledge', exemplified by another student's belief that 'it's all gonna be computers, isn't it'. Although computer skills are growing in importance in the labour-market, whether those competencies learned in a particular GCSE syllabus are valued by employers or, indeed, transferable from the classroom in any way, is less clear. In fact, educationalists and academics continue to debate such issues, and no consensus seems imminent (see Selwyn 1999).

This phenomena does not appear to be limited to one particular area of the curriculum, however. Indeed, Adey and Biddulph (2001) found similarly naïve views of the 'usefulness' of history and geography, both of which were viewed by large numbers of students as irrelevant to their future vocational aspirations.

There are two main issues arising from the examination of 'utility' as a motivation underlying choices in Year 9. First, some students, having no clear ideas about their future career intentions, appear to be employing strategies to ensure that their choice of GCSE subjects does not disadvantage them to any great extent, in terms of the number of future options available to them. Second, others appeared to view the 'utility' of different subjects in a hierarchical manner, with some subjects being considered more 'useful', in terms of labour market value, than others.

In the second part of this chapter these motivations are examined in terms of the frequency at which they arose and how they were distributed amongst the students. The issues discussed above are re-evaluated in light of this additional data.

The distribution of motivations

Table 5.1 shows the frequencies at which each type of motivation occurred among the student sample. Students providing one motivation are listed separate from those who listed two, to aid clarity.

Enjoyment

'Enjoyment' was cited by more students than any other motivation. Out of a total sub-sample of 48, only six students did not refer to 'enjoyment' at some point in their account of choices in Year 9. It was the most common sole reason for choices, accounting for 13 of the 16 cases where only one motivation was given. It was also the most frequently occurring category among those students who provided more than one motivation, with 29 of the 32 cases in this group referring to 'enjoyment' of a subject as important.

A key factor relating to students' 'enjoyment' of a subject is previous experience. It is possible, however, that owing to changes in the curriculum, for example, students' previous experience of a subject may not accurately reflect future experience and could therefore

Table 5.1 Year 9 choice motivations – by frequency

Motivation	**One motivation**	**Two motivations***
Enjoyment	13	29
Performance	0	18
Vocational	3	11
Utility	0	6
Total	**16**	**64**
No. of cases	16	32
Total no. of students (cases) = 48		

* *N.B.*: As each case accounts for *two* motivations, the total frequency of all motivations in this group is doubled. This is taken into consideration in the analysis that follows.

serve as a poor indicator of their future enjoyment. Previous research on educational choice has found that parents, when choosing secondary schools, tend to behave in a similar manner. They often base their choices on the past performance of an institution or the previous experience of another child, however dated this information may be, rather than conducting a current assessment or considering future developments (Gorard 1997).

There are also implications for subjects that are not offered before Key Stage 4. If many students choose subjects based on their previous experience they may be reluctant to opt for subject areas with which they are unfamiliar.

Performance

Academic performance was not mentioned by any of the students who gave only a single reason for their Year 9 choices. However, past performance in a subject was the second most common joint reason for decisions, with just over half (18/32) of the students who reported two motivations for their choices including it in their accounts. As with the category of 'enjoyment', it was not surprising to find that a considerable proportion of students (18/48) reported taking subjects in which they had previously performed well.

Vocational goals

It was surprising that very few students remembered considering any future career aspirations or expectations when choosing their Year 9 options. Only three out of the 16 students who provided only one reason for their choice referred to any longer-term plans, although it was the only reason other than 'enjoyment' given by this group. Slightly more than one-third (11/32) of those giving more than one reason mentioned vocational motivations. Overall, however, less than a third (14/48) of the sub-sample expressed overt commitment to post-16 destinations in their accounts of the Year 9 choice process.

Utility

'Utility' was the category cited least often by the students in justifications of their Year 9 choices, with only six out of the entire sub-sample (48) using such a rationale, always in conjunction with another reason. Interesting questions were raised, however, relating to the accuracy of their perceptions relating to the labour market value of particular qualifications. Investigating this area was beyond the scope of this study but constitutes an interesting topic for future research. Of equal interest are the sources of the information used to make such judgements

Motivations in combination

The ways in which categories of motivation were 'paired' is interesting. The first two categories, 'ability' and 'enjoyment' were often found within the same case, with half of the students who gave two reasons (16/32) mentioning 'enjoyment', the most commonly cited motivation by a large margin. It would be expected that it would also be the most likely to be 'paired' with any of the other categories and this is indeed the case. But it is important to note also that all 32 of the students who reported more than one reason specified either 'enjoyment' and/or 'ability', highlighting these concerns as central to decision making in Year 9. There were no other combinations of motivations that were noticeable in terms of their frequency. However, it is accepted that the relatively small number of cases may be partly responsible for obscuring any patterns.

Summary

There are several important issues raised in this chapter relating to the motivations underlying choices in Year 9. Some of these are specific to the choice process in that year but others resonate both with findings for other choice years and the conclusions drawn by other researchers examining educational choices.

Issues related to 'short-termism' regularly arose, and this could be seen as connecting the actions of the majority of students. Very few students had either future vocational plans or post-16 intentions in mind when choosing GCSE subjects in Year 9, and most simply chose the subjects they performed well in or enjoyed most.

In addition, students tended to judge their *future* educational experience according to *specific* experiences of their past schooling. Their past experiences, however, may not be representative of their future study. Either way, these assessments tend not to be based on reputable sources of information, such as subject teachers or career professionals. Notions regarding the 'utility' of some subjects (or their curriculum content) held by a few students also tended to be based on commonsense assumptions or 'folk knowledge' rather than any research conducted by the individuals concerned.

It should be restated here, however, that the data relating to choices made in Year 9 limits the scope for a meaningful analysis. As was discussed in Chapter 3, the topic of choices made before Year 11 was not a key concern when the research was originally conceived and was only incorporated because the students referred to it repeatedly in their interviews. Their descriptions of choices in this year were, however, shorter and less detailed than their accounts of decision making in Year 11. They also related to events that had taken place nearly two years previously. This should be borne in mind when the reading of the findings is being taken into consideration in the formulation of any conclusions.

In Chapter 6, motivations underlying choices in Year 11 are examined. Because of the higher quality of the data and the more complex nature of the choices faced, a more sophisticated taxonomy of motivations is developed.

6
Choice Factors and Rationales in Year 11

Introduction

As has already been discussed, the choice process in Year 11 is considerably more complex than in Year 9. At the end of compulsory schooling, students face a vast array of opportunities in terms of subjects, qualifications, courses and institutions. The motivations reported by the students as underlying the choices they had made are examined in detail in this chapter.

Factors, rationales and stages

Unlike the analysis of choices in Year 9 (see Chapter 5), the quality of the data relating to Year 11 choices allowed two dimensions of students' motivations to be differentiated, 'factors' and 'rationales'. These concepts are used in conjunction with the choice stages that were described in Chapter 4 and their interaction is explored later in this chapter. Before moving on to a more detailed examination of the data, the concepts are briefly defined.

For the purposes of the current analysis, 'factors' were defined as the elements of post-16 provision that students considered when making choices in Year 11. These include subject areas, qualifications, institutions, and so on. 'Rationales' were the explanations or justifications provided by students for either assigning priority to a particular 'factor' or deciding between alternative options in relation to a 'factor'. 'Rationales' included references to enjoyment, vocational considerations, higher education and convenience. In the sections below, each 'factor' is considered alongside the 'rationales' that accompanied them.

Qualification as a 'factor'

One of the factors appearing most frequently in students' accounts of their decision making in Year 11 was labelled 'qualification'. The majority of students made some reference to the type of qualification they hoped to study but several different rationales were provided to explain why they considered this particular factor to be important.

'Vocational' rationales

For some students the type of qualification (or qualifications) they intended to take was decided in a 'top-down' manner. The requirements of certain career paths (e.g. entering HE or pursuing particular occupations) often required a particular qualification type. Rationales such as these were coded as 'higher education' and 'vocational', respectively, and were sometimes provided in combination. Rationales relating to 'higher education' are examined later. The examples in this section connect the choice of qualification type (and often, as will be seen, *course* and *institution* type) to aspirations regarding relatively proximate labour market destinations. The students below describe how their vocational intentions influenced their choice of qualifications.

Redpost student male #6

Patrick White: And do you know what you are thinking of doing next year?

Student: Yes, I've got a good idea of what I'm going to do next year. [. . .] I'm going on to LumberTech to do a National Diploma or BTEC in Public Services.

Patrick White: Right. And what does that involve?

Student: It's nine hours of classroom work . . . five hours a week in the Army Cadets, police and riot-training and how to deal with the public . . . 'cos I'm hoping to go on to do customs and excise.

Gordon Cole student male #3

Student: Yes. I've sent in an application to Pondhill College . . . National Diploma in Countryside Management . . . that's what I want to do hopefully.

Gordon Cole student female #5

Patrick White: (. . .) So do you know what you're going to be doing next year?

Student: I'm hopefully going to Lincoln.

Patrick White: Lincoln?

Student: To do . . . it's part of the University of the Region of England . . . it's between Lumberton and Copperton . . . I don't know which way it is.

Patrick White: To do what?

Student: National Diploma in horse studies . . . because I want either to train police-horses or own a livery yard.

The three students above all intended to commit to a definite vocational direction at age 16. They were thus coded as having 'vocational' rationales for their choice of qualification, as the courses on which they hoped to enrol relate specifically to particular areas of work. Because of their specialist nature, their chosen occupational areas dictated not only the type of qualification required but also the institutions at which they could study. Because of this their choices were more tightly constrained compared to students who intended to take less specialised courses. All three students would have to travel considerable distances to attend institutions offering a suitable curriculum, and in one case this even meant living away from home. The decision to specialise so early was not common among the students in the sample. A number of students had at least some idea of their future career direction but very few planned to follow routes that would prevent them pursuing alternative directions should they change their minds.

As the above extracts demonstrate, it is not always straightforward to separate choices relating to subject areas, qualification types and institutions, as they are often interconnected. Because of this it is sometimes impossible to separate 'factors' into individual elements. Where separation became problematic, the 'factor' judged to be the most important to the student was recorded. This also has implications for the choice 'model' outlined in Chapter 4, as when choices are limited in this way separate choice 'stages' tend to be combined.

'Higher education' rationales

The desire to enter HE, separate from longer-term goals or occupational interest, was a rationale that was often linked to taking particular qualifications, usually A-levels or GNVQs. Given the trends in participation and course choice discussed in Chapter 3, this was not particularly surprising. The examples below raise a number of related issues.

Portland student male #4

Patrick White: Right. Those three A-levels you want to do, yeah, are there other courses other than A-levels you can take the subject to?

Student: Yeah, there's GNVQs you can do in business studies, and yeah, I was thinking about doing some of that, but you don't quite get the same sort of grades as A-level d'you?

Patrick White: Well, yeah it's different. (. . .) And d'you know what you are doing after you finish your A-levels ?

Student: I wouldn't mind going to university, I suppose. It'll depend on whether I get good enough grades . . . possibly Loughborough to do Sports.

This student has some ideas about possible HE courses but is not sure whether he will meet the entry requirements. This extract is the only example of a student raising the issue of 'parity of esteem' between A-levels and Advanced GNVQs. Indeed, many students appeared not to question the assumption that an Advanced GNVQ would be viewed by future 'gatekeepers' (i.e. employers or HE institutions) as equivalent to two A-levels.

Some students made 'default' choices regarding qualification type. Perhaps based on normative values originating from their familial and social background, they appeared never to have doubted the kind of course they would follow at the end of compulsory schooling.

Gordon Cole student male #4

Patrick White: So there was never any consideration that you might leave school at the end of the fifth year?

Student: No! No, no. Definitely do A-levels.

Patrick White: And are you thinking any further than that at the moment? Is that too far off?

Student: Yes.

Patrick White: Would you consider higher education as a possibility?
Student: Yes.

Kingfisher student male #8
Student: Only I thought . . . both my parents have been to university and stuff. I've always assumed that I'll probably follow in their footsteps, because they [parents] say it's essential to your life.

Although the first student states that he has not begun to consider seriously whether he would like to progress to HE, he claims that there was never any possibility that he would leave school at sixteen and he appears to have known for a long time that he would, or would at least be expected to, take A-levels. The second student took his 'assumptive trajectory' a step further, to include HE. A number of students adopted similar views, suggesting that these kinds of assumption are fairly common.

Occasionally, decisions relating to 'HE' and 'vocational' plans were not entirely separable in the students' narratives. For one student planning to enter dentistry, A-levels were necessary to gain a place on a suitable HE course.

Railroad student male #5
Patrick White: What sort of stuff d'you have to do?
Student: I need to get six GCSEs, and I need three A-levels, two A-levels in science and one in maths.
Patrick White: And then where d'you go from there?
Student: From there I'll go to college, get the A-levels, then I'll go to Cardiff University.

This particular student had carried out considerable research relating to his preferred career, including a detailed examination of the courses offered by different HE institutions. He clearly exemplifies an individual who used 'vocational' and 'higher education' rationales to explain his decisions regarding the qualifications he intended to take. The extent to which he had planned ahead was fairly unusual but several students in the sample constructed their choices according to similar rationales, particularly if they had long-standing ambitions to enter specific occupational areas. Most students' decisions, however, were based on much shorter-term plans and less clearly formulated ideas regarding eventual destinations.

Subject as a 'factor'

Subject areas played a major role in determining students' decisions concerning post-16 destinations. It was the factor reported most frequently in relation to decisions taking place during the 'primary' stage of the Year 11 choice process, perhaps indicating that it was foremost in students' minds at the outset of their decision making. It was often linked to vocational ambitions but, as was the case with GCSE options, a considerable number of students reported choosing subjects simply because they were interested in or enjoyed them. These two rationales also interacted, with some students pursuing certain vocational goals because they had enjoyed studying related subjects.

'Enjoyment' rationales

It was fairly common for students to report choosing subjects to study simply because they enjoyed them. This was the second most frequent rationale to be provided for subject choices, behind 'vocational' reasons. Perhaps unsurprisingly, 'enjoyment' rationales were only ever given in relation to choices relating to 'subject' and never connected to other factors by students. Indeed, it would be difficult for them to know whether they would enjoy qualifications and/or institutions that they had not experienced. In the extracts below students explain their choice of subjects according to this rationale.

Meadow Lane student male #2
Student: I mainly just sort of chose the stuff I liked.

Portland student male #4
Student: [. . .] I think I would have done the subjects that I wanted anyway.

Railroad student female #1
Student: I'm very enthusiastic about doing French and music, basically.
Patrick White: Mmm.

Student:	You know, I just like, went home as soon as I got the information pack about Railroad Sixth Form, and I said, 'Right, I'm going to Railroad sixth form and I'm doing French and music. Full stop!'

'Vocational' rationales

As was the case with students' choice of qualifications, 'vocational' rationales were often cited as being influential in relation to decisions regarding subject areas. The student below explains his vocational ambitions and how these affected his subject choices in Year 11.

Redpost student male #5

Patrick White:	So when you were choosing your subjects for college, was this with any longer-term goals in mind or was this just the next step?
Student:	Yes, I want to be a vet eventually . . . work with animals . . . that sort of thing.
Patrick White:	Right . . . OK.
Student:	That's why I chose the sciences and I chose the ones best for me.
Patrick White:	Which were . . . ?
Student:	Chemistry, biology and geography.
Patrick White:	Right.
Student:	I chose geography because if I fail to become a vet I can become a forester or whatever.
Patrick White:	So you want to be with nature?
Student:	Natural environment . . . animals and things.
Patrick White:	And is this something you've wanted to do for quite a long time?
Student:	Yes, we've always lived in the countryside . . . I've always wanted to work with animals and wild-life . . . stuff like that.

Although this student's principal aim is to become a veterinarian, his over-riding concern is to work with animals or in the countryside. He has chosen subjects (and a qualification type) that would allow him to pursue the first goal while not curtailing his options severely should he be unsuccessful in this. This kind of approach was more common than the early specialisation demonstrated by the three students in the previous section.

'Other' rationales

In a small-scale study, because of the small number of cases, it is not always possible to create meaningful categories for all types of behaviour. In relation to choice of subject there were two 'other' notable rationales that were reported by only a few students, and so were not incorporated into the general conceptual framework. They are described here, however, because of the issues they raise. A few students, despite having ideas about potential career destinations, professed a desire to keep their 'options open' with regard to future trajectories and report choosing their subjects accordingly.

Redpost student male #8

Patrick White: What about other people, do you think, I mean, for other areas of jobs, are your friends worried about . . .

Student: There's a lot of people that are not sure what they want to do. They're going into college and are picking three courses that are all different to each other . . .[to] keep their options open . . . they're not sure what they want to do.

Patrick White: Right, so they're . . . yeah . . . they haven't even thought much about it?

Student: I was like that in Year 9, not sure what I wanted to do . . . a vague idea . . . but there you go.

Portland school male #3

Patrick White: And do you know what subjects and courses you wanna do?

Student: Yes, maths, Further maths, physics and English.

Patrick White: Right, four then.

Student: Yes.

Patrick White: And that's all A-level.

Student: Yes.

Patrick White: Is that based around going on to do [computer] programming or some further course?

Student: Well it's really to give a good balance of subjects . . . I'm not too worried about a course in

Programming as such. I mean I'll have to see what's available at university, but one of my thoughts is to get a good maths degree and, you know, then I'll have the option of going into lots of different jobs if the programming doesn't work out.

The way in which these students describe their choice behaviour (or, in the case of the second student, their friends' choice behaviour) suggests that some young people, although not certain about future occupational destinations while still in Year 11, are concerned to make sure that they leave further education with subjects and/or qualifications that are marketable in labour market terms.

This concern with the relative value of particular subjects and the coherence of particular subject combinations recurred in a slightly different context in relation to subject choices. As it had done in relation to GCSE options in Year 9, the currency of certain subjects in terms of future labour market and/or higher education prospects was raised by some students. The two students below report parental concern in this area.

Portland student female #2

Student: That's why my mum didn't want me to do theatre studies, and she doesn't think it's, sort of, an accepted A-level, which I can understand.

Meadow Lane student female #2

Patrick White: So what are you planning to do next year?

Student: English literature, history and biology. I'm undecided about a third . . . or a fourth . . . I might either do a fourth A-level or an AS. I'm definitely going to have three and a half.

Patrick White: In what?

Student: I'm not really sure yet, it's either going to be in music, religious studies or chemistry, or possibly psychology. I'd like to do psychology, but my parents don't want me to do it.

Patrick White: Why?

Student: I think it's because it's like a new subject, they don't know what it involves and also because my mum

> did it as part of her English literature degree course and she didn't like it. It was all sort of like reception in new-born babies and said it was really frustrating, so . . .

Again, like the issue of 'parity of esteem', this topic was only raised by a very small number of students. On these occasions it clearly originated from parental intervention but, nevertheless, prompted concern on the part of the students involved. The two extracts are also interesting for another, related reason. *Portland student female #2* appears to sympathise with the position taken by her mother, claiming to understand her views on the status of theatre studies in relation to other subjects. Previous research has encountered similar views regarding 'new' subject areas. Richards (2005), for example, reports that media studies was not always regarded as a legitimate area of study by the parents of the young people in his study. As was shown in Chapter 3, however, 'new' subjects have become increasingly popular in recent years, at the expense of enrolments in more traditional areas.

Because such issues were not addressed by the vast majority of students, it is difficult to draw any broad conclusions. These issues would not be relevant to many students, as the subjects and/or qualifications they intended to take were well established. However, although a substantial minority of students had chosen either vocational courses or 'new' subject areas, very few students appeared to be aware of these debates.

Institution as a 'factor'

Of all the factors students described, choice of institution gave rise to the widest range of rationales. Excluding those classified as 'other', four different types of rationale were mentioned. Most of the responses, however, fitted into either the 'academic/organisational' or 'travel/convenience' categories. The rationales connected with this factor are examined below.

'Academic/organisational' rationales

The most common rationale given by students to justify their choice of institution was labelled 'academic/organisational'. These included any references to the academic outcomes of a school or college, its organisation and/or structure, facilities and the teaching staff employed. Although this rationale includes a diverse range of issues, these all relate to the social organisation of institutions.

The student below justifies his decision to stay at his present institution primarily in relation to the academic 'performance' of the school.

Portland student male #3

Student:	(. . .) I mean, I think they get pretty much the best A-level results in the area here, so I just don't see the point [of going anywhere else].
Patrick White:	So that's your main consideration the sort of A-level results, or were you just happy to be here?
Student:	Partly the results, partly I'm happy to be here.
Patrick White:	What do your parents think about that then? Did they just assume you'd just stay?
Student:	Yes, I think so.
Patrick White:	Right. It kind of seems like a natural progression.
Student:	Yes.
Patrick White:	Doesn't seem any reason for going anywhere else.
Student:	No.

It was not uncommon for students to refer to the academic performance of particular institutions in their accounts of choosing a post-16 destination. However, none of the students appealing to this type of rationale referred to any official sources of information. Their beliefs regarding the relative 'performance' of institutions appeared to be based mainly on the local reputations of the schools and colleges involved. The language used by students also suggested that they were unsure of the claims they were making. In the extract above, *Portland student male #3* stated that he 'thought' *Portland* achieved the highest A-level results in the area. Although such information is published yearly in local newspapers, no students talked about 'league tables' or any other indicators of institutional 'performance'. Indeed, previous research on secondary school choice reports similar behaviour, in terms of both students' omission of references to information sources (Smedley 1995) and the tendency of students *and* their parents to judge according to 'local reputation' (West and Varlaam 1991).

Another area drawn upon by students deciding on a particular institution relates to the organisation or structure of an institution. The extract below illustrates a common theme.

Meadow Lane student female #2
Patrick White: Do you want to go to Davchester College?
Student: I would like to, I'm not sure if I'm going to or not. [I'm] looking at Chalfont College, Chalfont Boys' College. 'Cause they're going co-ed next year.
Patrick White: What are your parents' thoughts about that?
Student: They would rather I went there than Davchester College. They think I need a change and a stronger structure.

This student, along with many others in the sample, made comparisons between the way that school sixth forms and 'colleges' (they did not distinguish between FE colleges and tertiary colleges) were 'organised' or 'structured'. Their perceptions of the differences between the 'two types' of institution concentrated on the regimes of surveillance, regulation and control which operated within them. As in the above extract, parents were often responsible both for initially raising the issue and for providing the 'relevant' information. With only one exception, parental concern appeared to focus on the apparent *laissez-faire* approach to both surveillance and regulation believed to be characteristic of any institution to which the label 'college' could be applied. Again, the grounding of their judgements tended to be expressed in rather vague terms and were often based on inaccurate information. The student below describes her views at some length.

Portland student female #2
Patrick White: Would you be prepared to go somewhere else if you couldn't do what you wanted to do?
Student: Yes. I did consider doing Spanish somewhere else. When you look at the College a lot of the lecturers . . .
Patrick White: That's Davchester [Tertiary] College?
Student: Yes, Davchester College. A lot of the lecturers aren't just lecturers, they either lecture elsewhere as well

or they have jobs and they are a lot more open-minded. A lot of teachers, I think, go straight through education and they've never worked in industry or with people, they've always worked with young people and they treat you so . . . Miss Grater makes me feel so small, and she won't speak to you like another person. She still calls us children even when she's speaking French, she calls us children, and it's so patronising, I can't stand it.

Patrick White: So you think that college might offer a more . . .

Student: Yes, a more adult atmosphere.

Patrick White: What about . . . ?

Student: Self discipline?

Patrick White: How did you know what I was going to say?

Student: [laughs] 'Cos that's something that comes up with me and I probably . . . I don't know whether I'd get the work done or not, but at least it would be off my own bat.

Patrick White: Do you think it might actually be a positive step, the fact that you are suddenly left on your own and that you might almost panic yourself into getting it done?

Student: I suppose, yes. I mean, it's not the teachers that I'm worried about, it's the fact that here they register the sixth form and everything [at Portland], so they chase you up if you skip lessons, whereas in Davchester College they don't chase you for 'cuts' apparently[. . .] The other thing is that I would worry about going to somewhere like Davchester College would be how willing my mum would be to let me have the freedom.

This extract raises new issues as well as repeating some of the views expressed by *Meadow Lane student female #2*. The second student speculates on some of the advantages of attending a 'college' and also makes assumptions regarding the pedagogical culture of such institutions. As before, these views are unsupported by any reliable source of information. This student is not entirely sure how she would fare in such circumstances but, like the previous case, feels that her parents would be concerned. Although anxieties regarding attendance and subsequent performance, especially on the part of parents, were regularly reported by interviewees, interviews with teaching staff at the institutions concerned gave the impression that these fears were largely unfounded.

These accounts, however, offer an important insight into what some parents want for their children. Their wishes in this case fit remarkably well with what Gorard (1997) calls the 'reflection effect', a desire that their child have a similar educational experience to their own. Their perceptions regarding the kind of education provided in a 'college' may be explained in relation to their own experiences two or three decades previously, when the main alternative to a sixth form education (apart from entering the labour force) was to attend a 'technical college' to engage in vocational training. However, although their views of the differences between the institutions may be inaccurate, the fact that their desire for education centred on 'traditional' values provides clues to the origin of their concerns and also their misconceptions regarding the organisation of some types of contemporary post-16 institutions.

A rationale that was also included in the 'academic/organisational' category, and that is related in some ways to the structure and organisation of an institution, is 'continuity'. Some students explained their decisions to stay at their present institution (usually an 11–18 school) in terms of minimising disruption to their studies.

Railroad student male #5

Patrick White: So, are you going to stay here next year, to do the A-levels?

Student: Yeah. I think so. 'Cause I said . . . if I change to another school, you've got, like, gotta wait half a year, so you get settled in, *then* you start learning. So I thought if I stay here, I'm already settled in.

Patrick White: Mmm. Is that something that you've just thought about?

Student: That's what I've been told by my science teacher.

Patrick White: Oh, right. Yeah. So, if you were going somewhere else would it be the college [Dean FE], or would you go to Davchester?

Student: Yeah, probably one of them two.

Patrick White: Right. But you're not really considering it?
Student: No.

In this case, the idea that changing institutions at the end of Year 11 would negatively affect learning was suggested to the student by a subject teacher. This advice appeared to have some influence on the student's actions as, at the time of interview, he was no longer seriously considering attending any alternative post-16 institutions. Whether he would have still been considering alternative destinations had the discussion not taken place is open to speculation. It is interesting that it was a subject teacher, rather than careers teacher or officer, who provided this advice. Previous research has tended to focus on the influence of careers professionals on decisions in Year 11, and while some researchers (e.g. Taylor 1992; Foskett and Hesketh 1997) have documented cases where teachers have been influential, these are not particularly common.

Another type of 'organisational' or 'structural' rationale for choosing post-16 destinations related to the facilities provided by post-16 institutions. This was most important for students intending to take 'resource-heavy' courses in subjects such as art, sciences and computer studies. The student below describes her choice to study art at an alternative post-16 institution.

Railroad student female #4
Patrick White: D'you want to do that here?
Student: Not art here. I'm doing art at the College.
Patrick White: So you can do that?
Student: Yeah.
Patrick White: I mean, could've you done art here?
Student: I could do art here, yeah.
Patrick White: And the College isn't that far?
Student: The College is just down the road. But the A-level campus, for art, is in Tackley. Which is actually good. I mean, it's a whole . . . it used to be a secondary school. It's like . . . the whole school, and they've turned it into an art school.
Patrick White: Is that why you want to go there, for the facilities?
Student: Yeah. Yeah.

This student's rather unusual decision to split her post-16 provision between two institutions has been discussed previously, in Chapter 4. Specialist resources are not equally distributed between institutions and, as Payne (2003) notes, the courses and facilities offered by different providers can impact on young people's choice of post-16 destination.

'Travel/convenience' rationales

Because of the relatively rural location of all the schools in the sample, it had been predicted that travel considerations would play a major role in determining students' post-16 destinations. Rationales relating to 'travel' and 'convenience' were used by some students to explain their choice of post-16 educational institution, although the total number (12) was much smaller than originally anticipated.

The student below describes some of the problems that can arise as a result of geographical isolation combined with irregular public transport.

Portland student female #3

Patrick White: So . . . Oh right, so you are wanting to do A-levels, yeah?

Student: Yeah . . . stay on here.

Patrick White: You don't fancy trying somewhere else . . . seeing as you're used to moving around?

Student: [laughs] I can't get anywhere else really . . . it's a bit patchy, not having a bus which goes to Gifford or Davchester.

Patrick White: You have to get a lift in to Danford or . . .

Student: Yeah . . . my mum says if I wanted to go to Davchester I'd have to bike into Danford every day . . . and I thought well, in the winter . . .

Patrick White: Did you ever think about it? Or did you assume you just wouldn't be able to get there?

Student: I did think about Davchester, but I didn't fancy being by myself, 'cos I know a lot of people here . . . and I've got my friends . . . none of my friends are going to Davchester.

Patrick White: So are they all staying here?
Student: Yeah . . . it'd be easier if I stayed here . . . and I get on with the teachers.

This interviewee initially frames her decision to remain at her present institution in terms of the difficulty of travelling to an alternative institution. She cites the lack of public transport as the main problem, stating that she 'can't get anywhere else really'. However, later in her account it becomes apparent that she has discussed the possibility of attending Davchester College, the nearest alternative post-16 institution. It transpires that her mother would not (or could not) give her a lift to Danford every morning to catch the bus to Davchester, so that she would have to cycle.

The extract below shows another student who weighs up the advantages and disadvantages of attending an alternative post-16 institution.

Meadow Lane student male #3
Patrick White: And have you considered going anywhere else apart from Davchester College?
Student: I suppose I thought about it, but . . . I only live down the road really and I was thinking that if I have to travel somewhere for half an hour travelling and then half an hour at night, that's an extra hour I could spend doing work, sort of thing.
Patrick White: Mmm . . .
[. . .]
Student: Yes, and then I've got an awful lot of course work to do.
Patrick White: Mmm. So what other options would there be?
Student: Erm . . . there's a couple of sixth-form colleges . . . there's Portland, Knightshead . . . there's the colleges in Dean.
Patrick White: But they're all quite a distance from here?
Student: They're all about ten miles away from here really.

This student, whose preferred courses are all offered at his local institution, sees little point in changing to an alternative post-16 provider. He believes that the time spent travelling could be better spent studying and, as his chosen courses involve a great deal of coursework, this issue is of particular concern. Although he mentions the costs in terms of time, he does not refer to the additional financial expense usually incurred as a result of travel. It is interesting that few students made any references to the economic consequences of their choices. This may result from the social make-up of the sample (see Chapter 3) but even students from 'lower' occupational class backgrounds, such as example illustrated directly below, rarely commented on financial issues. Financial constraints were certainly never given as the *sole* rationale behind institutional choice. It may be that students were reluctant to mention financial hardship because of embarrassment or that they had not considered the cumulative cost of travel arrangements to and from post-16 institutions. In any case, this topic was noticeably absent from their accounts.

Perhaps the most obvious example of the effect travel considerations can have on vocational trajectories is the case of the student below.

Railroad student female #5

Patrick White: Had you considered going anywhere else, like to the FE college or Davchester or LumberTech or anything?

Student: I was gonna go to LumberTech to do a Health and Beauty course. But then it was just the fact of me getting there in the mornings and getting back and everything. So I just thought I might as well stay on at Railroad, cause I know Railroad. Been here for five years, so . . . might as well . . . stay here.

Although it would have been possible for this student to travel to the institution which offered her preferred course, she eventually decided to remain at Railroad School to attend the sixth form there. A consequence of this decision was that she would no longer be able to take a course in Health and Beauty, settling instead for doing a Health and Social Care GNVQ. This change from a specialised vocational course to a more general one could possibly have implications for her career trajectory in the short term, as while the former course is directed at preparation for entry into a specific occupational area, the latter is not. In this case, a particular occupational goal may have been forfeited (or delayed) because of reasons relating to travel.

It is noticeable that this student provides a secondary rationale to justify her choice. Having decided not to change institution at the end of Year 11, she appeals to her familiarity with her current school. This is a common theme running through many of the students' accounts of decisions to remain in their present institutions. In contrast, there are few examples of students wanting to change institutions to experience a new one and to meet different people (but see *Gordon Cole student female #5* below). This is also true for students using 'academic' rationales. Although such rationales were frequently used to defend the choice to stay at an institution, they were used less often to justify moving to an alternative post-16 provider.

Two central themes have arisen in this discussion of rationales relating to 'travel' and/or 'convenience'. The importance of parental involvement in many students' accounts reflects the findings of previous studies in the area (e.g. Taylor 1992; Furlong 1993; Foskett and Hesketh 1997). This can often be expressed through setting parameters of what they consider to be acceptable subjects, qualifications or institutions. However, as was seen in the first extract (*Portland student female #3*), parents can wield considerable power when private transport is needed in order to attend a particular post-16 institution, an especially important factor in rural areas.

A second theme concerns students' post-16 mobility in terms of educational institutions. There appears to be a tendency to attend the nearest post-16 institution or stay at an 11–18 school even if there are particular advantages to be gained from enrolling elsewhere. Sometimes students will even forfeit the course required to enter their preferred vocational field rather than change institution, as is demonstrated by the case of *Railroad student female #5*. Of course, there are often very good reasons to attend the local post-16 institution (see *Meadow Lane student male #3,* for example) and as Payne (1995) has noted, the easiest course of action for students is simply to 'stay put'. However some of the possible advantages of attending alternative institutions, such as providing a 'half-way house' before moving on to HE, were rarely raised by students and appeared only very occasionally to influence their decisions.

'Social' rationales

Another rationale expected to feature prominently in students' accounts related to 'social' reasons for choosing an institution. In fact, only five students in total broached the subject, four mentioning it in combination with another rationale. It may be that students were reluctant to provide rationales which might be perceived by figures of authority (such as an interviewer) as 'unacceptable' or 'undesirable'. However, there was little evidence to suggest that most interviewees were anything but completely honest in their responses. Indeed, some of the students were frank about wanting to stay with their friends or go where most of their peer group were planning to attend. However, the possibility remains that some students were not as forthright.

The most straightforward example of the impact of 'social' considerations on a student's choice of post-16 institution is illustrated directly below.

Gordon Cole student female #2

Patrick White: And do you want to stay here?

Student: Yes.

Patrick White: And they are going to let you stay here?

Student: I hope so, yes! [laughs]

Patrick White: You expect that they will then, yes?

Student: I think so, yes. I'm having an interview at Davchester College. I went there on the Open Day . . . it was quite good but a lot of my friends are staying here so I'll probably end up staying here 'cos I'm not a very confident, outgoing person. [I'm] not very good at making new friends . . . so, I'll stay here.

Patrick White: Security?

Student: Yes.

Although she considered an alternative institution, this student decided to stay at school because she felt she was 'not very good at making new friends' and would find moving to another institution very difficult. It was fairly common for students to report having considered changing institutions before but deciding against it, both for 'social' and other reasons. The student below, however, is a rare example of a young person (from the same school as the previous student) actively seeking to change her environment.

Gordon Cole student female #5

Patrick White: OK . . . why Davchester College?

Student:	Well, I don't want to stay here 'cos I don't want to be around with little first-years . . . make a new start. That's why I think Lincoln will be a good opportunity . . . because it's residential . . . two years.
Patrick White:	Yes . . . oh, right.
Student:	Make new friends.

This student's rationale is very different to the previous one, as she reported wanting to change institutions to make new friends rather than remain with her present ones. She embraced all aspects of the transition to a different environment as part of making a 'new start' that may even include moving away from home. She also makes reference to what might be considered an 'organisational' influence, the age composition of the students in the college. This was not mentioned by any other participants, although some students referred to their desire for an 'adult atmosphere'. This, however, tended to relate to interaction with staff rather than other students.

'Vocational' rationales

As was the case with rationales relating to qualification type discussed earlier in this chapter, the institution that students decided to attend was sometimes dictated by the course they intended to study. The pursuit of particular vocational directions frequently dictated the appropriate qualification and course which, in turn, limited the possible number of institutional destinations. In cases where students were interested in specific, proximate, vocational destinations the choice of both qualification, course and institution were often inseparable. Students pursuing such a direction tended not to negotiate all of the three choice stages outlined in Chapter 4, as the number of choices they made were restricted by their particular preferences. The extracts provide illustrate examples of this phenomenon.

Redpost student male #6

Patrick White:	And do you know what you are thinking of doing next year?
Student:	Yes, I've got a good idea of what I'm going to do next year. It's basically been influenced by first of all TV . . . and then basically having a good long

hard think about it. And if I get four Cs [at GCSE] and above, I'm going on to LumberTech and do a National Diploma or BTEC in public services.

Patrick White: Right, and what does that involve?

Student: It's nine hours of classroom work, five hours a week in the army cadets, police and riot-training and how to deal with the public, 'cos I'm hoping to go on to do customs and excise.

Patrick White: Right, so that's a kind of course that prepares you for the services of police and all that kind of thing?

Student: Dealing with the public.

Patrick White: Oh right. Is that a new course?

Student: It's . . . I don't know. I assume they've still got it on trial because there's only twenty places at LumberTech . . . It doesn't go on at Davchester or Dean . . . or Lincoln or places like that. I just wanted to stay in Lumbertonshire basically. I didn't really want to go to Gifford . . . there's a couple of people from our school that I know who are going there.

This student had very specific vocational aspirations and planned to enrol on a specialist course at a large FE college, the only institution in the LEA offering the required course. The largest of its kind in Lumbertonshire and offering many vocational courses unavailable elsewhere in the county, this college had close links with a nearby HE institution. As such, it was a popular choice for students with definite occupational goals requiring early specialisation and training, and also more general vocational qualifications. The institution described by the student in the next extract, however, is of a very different kind.

Gordon Cole student male #3

Student: It's more into the farming side . . . agriculture and that sort of thing.

Patrick White: Is that something that you might be interested in doing?

Student: Yes. I've sent in an application to Waterdale College . . . National Diploma in countryside management . . . that's what I want to do hopefully.

Patrick White: What, after this year?
Student: Yes.
Patrick White: Right, and is that somewhere fairly near?
Student: Yes, it's about fifteen miles away. It's by Hensham.
Patrick White: Where . . . Hensham. And is that the nearest [place] you can do that sort of thing?
Student: Yes, Lincoln is the other agricultural college. They say it's your local one but it's miles away really. Hensham's a lot nearer . . . it's just in Valeshire . . . we're just on the outskirts.

This is a clear example of a choice of institution being limited by the availability of suitable courses. There are only two agricultural colleges within reasonable travelling distance of this student's home and he chose the nearest one. However, this is not the institution referred to by other students who had similar aspirations. Indeed, this student reports that his contemporaries were misled about the proximity of the two institutions. It is unclear, however, why the advice given by careers professionals conflicted with the information available to this student.

In the extract below a student makes a rather uncommon choice regarding his post-16 destination.

Kingfisher student male #4
Patrick White: And so what do you think you'll be doing next year?
Student: When I was out on the second of the two engineering things . . . they talked about the SET which is the Smallpiece Engineering Trainingship . . . and I'm really interested in that . . . I'm filling in my application at the moment.
Patrick White: Right, and where will you be doing that?
Student: That's in Coventry.
Patrick White: Right, so you'll have to move away?
Student: Yes.

This student is unusual for two reasons. Apart from the fact that he is one of the few students who has decided to specialise vocationally in

Year 12 he is also an example of two even less typical Year 11 choices. First, the occupational area he plans to enter (engineering) is not mentioned by any other student in the sample. It represents a serious commitment to a vocational pathway, as any subsequent changes would result in considerable disruption. Whilst in the 1960s and 1970s young people routinely committed themselves to apprenticeships (the closest contemporary comparator) at age fifteen or sixteen, such behaviour is much less common today in a social and economic climate characterised by 'prolonged transitions to uncertain destinations' (Roberts 1997b, p. 345). In addition to this, he also elected to enrol on a residential course. Considering the possibility of attending a residential institution was certainly not an option reported as considered by many students (but see Gordon Cole student female #5, earlier). Indeed, many were reluctant to even consider leaving school to attend a local college.

The distribution of factors and rationales

Having illustrated the various factors and rationales that appeared in the students' narratives, the frequency with they interact is investigated. Factors and rationales are also examined in relation to the choice stages within which they occur, demonstrating how the concepts developed in the last two chapters can be integrated with the 'choice models' developed in Chapter 4.

Choice factors and choice stages

Table 6.1 shows the relationship between the choice factors considered by students and the choice stage in which these took place. There is a strong link between the different factors and the stages of the Year 11 choice process in which they were most likely to be addressed. It appears that most students made decisions about the subject or subjects they wished to study in the primary stage of the choice process. Choices relating to 'qualification' were most likely to take place in the secondary choice stage and institutions tended to be chosen in the tertiary stage. Analysis of individual cases also revealed that this was the most common sequence of decisions.

It is entirely plausible, however, that the pattern observed in Table 6.1 is an artefact of the data collection and data analysis. Students may have tended to discuss their choices first in terms of

Table 6.1 Choice factors and choice stages

Choice factors:	Choice stages			
	Primary	**Secondary**	**Tertiary**	***Total***
Subject	33	11	8	52
Qualification	11	35	5	51
Institution	7	6	39	52
Other/comb	2	1	1	4
				159
Number of cases	53	53	53	

subjects, then qualifications, and lastly institutions. This might then have led to the decisions tending to be categorised as 'primary', 'secondary' and 'tertiary' in terms of the order in which they were raised by students. However, if this was the case, the question of why students tended to raise these three factors in this particular order is raised. Nevertheless, the data displayed in Table 6.3 demonstrates, at the very least, strong patterns in the ways that young people articulate their choices after the fact, an important finding in itself.

If these findings were replicated in a larger-scale study, they could be used to inform careers education and guidance (CEG) provision leading up to post-16 transitions. Interventions could be organised in the knowledge that students most commonly approach the choices they face in Year 11 in a particular sequence and the foci of CEG provision could then be structured so as to address issues in a way that corresponds to this sequence. This might not be ideal for all or even the majority of students but may be more effective than curricula arranged along more arbitrary lines.

Factors and rationales

The relationships between choice factors and the rationales behind such choices have already been discussed earlier in this chapter. These were illustrated with extracts from student interviews and were occasionally accompanied by frequencies in order to convey the incidence of particular links. In previous discussions, however, data relating to all cases were not presented consistently or systematically. This section presents this information in order to provide an

Table 6.2 The relationship between factors and rationales: all students

Choice rationale:	Choice factor Institution	Qualification	Subject	Other	Total
Enjoyment	0	0	24	0	24
Travel/convenience	12	0	0	0	12
Vocational	2	37	42	3	84
Higher education	0	33	7	0	40
Social	5	0	0	1	6
Academic/org.	38	0	0	0	38
Other	4	6	7	2	19
Total*	61	76	80	6	
No. of cases	48	54	54	5	
Total no. students					59

* Totals differ according to the number of students providing one or two rationales for the choice of each factor.

overview of how these concepts were distributed among the student sample.

Table 6.2 shows the total number of rationales given by students in relation to any one choice factor. There are clear links between particular factors and rationales.

It must be considered, however, that the input of students who provided two rationales relating to a single factor is over-represented at the expense of those who only provided one. Students participating in only two choice stages are also under-represented, as is the case with Table 6.1. However, presenting the data separately for these groups of students would not have changed the observed patterns to any great extent.

Institutional choices

When considering the choice of an institution (or institutions) 'academic/organisational' rationales were most likely to be used to justify the eventual decision. In fact, there were 38 instances of such rationales in the 59 accounts of post-16 choice. 'Travel/convenience' rationales were the second most frequently cited rationales, with 12 instances. There were also occasional references to 'social' (5) and 'vocational' (2) rationales.

As noted earlier, that 'academic/organisational' rationales were commonly used to explain institutional choices is not surprising. All such rationales related to aspects of the organisation or structure of an institution, or features that students perceived to be intrinsic to particular institutions, including aggregated academic outcomes. What was remarkable, however, was the extent to which these rationales dominated the students' responses. 'Academic/organisational' responses accounted for nearly two-thirds (38/61) of all the rationales given for institutional choice. The next most popular rationale, 'travel/convenience', represented less than one-fifth (12/61) of the total responses. And as can be seen from the Table 6.2, only two other rationales were mentioned, accounting for 11 responses.

Travel was a consideration for some students, although fewer than had been expected, given the rural nature of the area and the poor level of public transport provision. Less than one-fifth of the rationales provided by students were coded in the 'travel/convenience' category. 'Social' rationales were also raised much less frequently than had been expected, representing only 5 out of the total 61 rationales.

Qualification choices

Only two rationales (apart from six cases coded as 'other') were given by students in relation to their choices of qualification or qualifications, those categorised as relating to 'vocational' goals or entry to 'higher education'. The frequency of their occurrence (37 and 33, respectively) was very similar, perhaps because routes into employment and higher education often require particular qualifications. However, few students discussed the relative 'status' of different qualifications. This suggests that they may be isolated from, or indifferent to, the continuing debate regarding the 'parity of esteem' of qualification types, particularly those characterised as 'vocational' and 'academic'.

Subject choices

Students primarily appealed to 'vocational' rationales to explain their subject choices. These accounted for over half (42/80) of all rationales relating to this factor. In addition, between one-quarter and one-third (24/80) of the rationales fell into the category of 'enjoyment'. Only 7 out of 80 rationales related to 'higher education'.

Rationales relating to 'enjoyment' were expected to feature more prominently in the students' narratives. As with all these analytic constructs, however, it is possible, that such rationales were subsumed within other categories. For example, students intending to follow particular career paths into higher education and/or the labour market may frame their explanations in relation to these, even though their enjoyment of a related subject area was the original motivation for their interest in this trajectory. Such motivations may have become 'embedded' within students' worldviews and never articulated in their accounts of their career choices. Indeed, Heath (2002) documented a similar phenomenon in her research relating to post-16 choice and language. Nevertheless, rationales fitting into the 'enjoyment' category accounted for over one-quarter of the explanations of subject choices and remain an important feature of the decision-making process for a large minority of the students.

'Higher education' rationales also featured less prominently than anticipated but, again, could have been subsumed within 'vocational' explanations. Students appeared to be aware of the qualification types required for HE entry but often ignored the limitations that subject combinations taken in post-16 education could place on the kind of route they take *through* the HE system.

Summary

Rationales similar to all those examined in this chapter have been documented in previous studies. The popularity of 'academic/organisational' rationales for the choice of a particular institution reflects the similar but perhaps more specific observation that course choice and institutional choice are often linked (Foskett and Hesketh 1997; Keys *et al.* 1998; Taylor 1992). The connection between subject choice and enjoyment observed in the present study was also found by Fitz-Gibbon (1997). The continuing importance of 'vocational' goals and/or the intention to enter 'higher education' is demonstrated by the similarity of the findings discussed above and those of studies conducted at various points over the past 30 years (e.g. Vincent and Dean 1977; Taylor 1992; Keys *et al.* 1998).

As in previous studies, very few of the students' decisions were articulated in terms of long-term goals. For example Taylor (1992), in a much larger-scale study, found that most young people had only very vague ideas about the occupations they might pursue in the future. However, a small minority of young people in the present study had very clear occupational ambitions and, correspondingly detailed plans relating to their post-16 destinations. Nevertheless, most students appeared to be prepared to defer any such decisions for at least a year or two.

An interesting and unexpected finding related to the issue of 'parity of esteem' between qualification types. Very few students referred to the relative status of vocational and academic qualifications at all. No concerns were expressed regarding the value of vocational qualifications in terms of either entry to the labour market or higher education. It is difficult to make conclusions based on the absence of a particular issue in the students' accounts but this finding is certainly worth recording. It is particularly interesting in light of the fact that the relative value of different subjects was discussed. Concerns in this area invariably originated discussions with parents, who occasionally expressed doubts about the value of subjects they characterised as 'new', such as theatre studies and psychology. However, some 'new' subjects, such as business studies, were not questioned in the same way, perhaps suggesting that perceived vocational relevance, rather than their longevity, was the primary concern.

The beliefs that students and their parents held in relation to the 'transformative capacities' of educational institutions was also revealed. Most young people in the study clearly thought that the post-16 institution they attended could fundamentally affect their performance and subsequent academic outcomes. While this idea appeals to a 'common sense' rationality that is easy to understand, and there is some evidence to suggest that there may be an 'institutional effect' in terms of staying-on rates (Cheng 1995; Payne 1998), the 'school effectiveness' literature would suggest that any institutional impact on academic outcomes would be negligible (Gorard 2000).

Some parents were also reported to hold strong, but perhaps unfounded, views about particular types of post-16 institutions. Students frequently reported parental concern regarding the regimes of surveillance, regulation and control operated at what they referred to as 'colleges'. When questioned on this matter, however, the interviewees often knew very little about even the number of types of FE providers in the area, let alone any specific detail about how they were organised. Importantly, however, the impressions of particular institutions held by students and their parents often influenced their decisions.

Students also displayed a tendency to remain in their present institutions, if at all possible. Students appeared reluctant to change institutions even when they acknowledged and/or articulated beneficial reasons for doing so, and rationales used to remain at their current school were seldom used to justify moving to an alternative institution. This reflects the national trends examined in Chapter 2, which confirm that most students in schools with sixth forms who continue with full-time education do so at their current institution. And as Payne (1995) has noted, it is much easier for them to do this than to move elsewhere.

The analytic strategy used in the present study allowed the interview data to be subject to further interrogation. The distribution of the 'factors' and 'rationales' was recorded, as was their interaction and also the interaction between the 'factors' and 'choice stages'. Whilst any conclusions drawn from these analyses must necessarily be tentative, some relationships emerged of sufficient strength to be taken seriously.

Links were established between the factors students considered when making decisions about their post-16 options and the particular rationales used to explain their choices. Subject choices were most frequently supported by 'vocational' rationales, qualification choices by either 'vocational' or 'higher education' rationales and institutional choices by 'academic/organisational' rationales. These findings are similar to those of previous studies in the area, reinforcing the links between particular choices and the reasoning behind them.

More interestingly, the analysis of the interaction between the choice factors and choice stages suggested that particular factors tended to be associated with each of the three choice stages that make up the Year 11 choice process. Most students appeared to make decisions concerning subjects first, in the primary choice stage. In the secondary stage they were most likely to consider qualification types and in the tertiary stage institutional choice was most commonly addressed. As can be seen by comparing Tables 6.1 and 6.2, these patterns are clearly connected to the relationship between factors and rationales. If these phenomena could be demonstrated to be more widespread there may be implications for the provision of guidance relating to post-16 transitions. This finding also raises questions about the nature of educational choice more widely and whether decisions relating to, for example, HE are made in a similar manner. This is a question that future researchers may wish to address.

In Chapter 3, the 'mechanism' of the choice process in Year 11 was described. The present chapter developed the model, showing how the students' choice factors and rationales were structured within this framework. Relationships appear to exist between the different choice factors and associated types of rationale and these, in turn, are connected to the various choice stages constructed earlier in the analysis. In Chapter 7 the role played by students' occupational aspirations will be examined.

7 Destinations, Aspirations and Trajectories

Over the course of the last three chapters, the nature of the students' choices, the factors they considered important, and the rationales behind their choices have all been examined. However, as was discussed in Chapter 1, the occupational aspirations and expectations of the young people are a central concern, as the extent to which they influence choices may increase our understanding of the decision-making process. This chapter examines these aspirations and expectations and their relationship to the choices made by the students.

Occupational aspirations

Although, at the time of interview, most students had committed to particular post-16 destinations, fewer than half (27/59) could provide any indication of occupational areas they might be interested in pursuing. Given previous research in the area (e.g. Taylor 1992) this is not surprising but it does limit the possibilities for meaningful analysis of this subject.

There are also problems inherent in examining the occupational aspirations of young people at this point in their lives. As most students planned to complete at least one year of post-compulsory education and/or training before entering the labour market, occupational intentions usually related to destinations that would only be realised quite some time in the future. Indeed, those planning to enter higher education would be unlikely to enter the labour market for at least five years. The issue of how closely any career goals expressed in Year 11 relate to *actual* future destinations is a question that is immediately raised.

The issue of the accuracy of young people's perceptions of the day-to-day realities of particular occupations is also important, as it is the source of any information used. There was evidence to suggest that some young people, while claiming to have particular occupational aspirations, had not even given much thought to their suitability for the area of work concerned. The student below exemplifies this, albeit in a somewhat exaggerated form.

Railroad student female #2

Student: Leisure and Tourism is because I wanna get involved in the tourist industry and sort of travelling. I'm not really sure what pacific [sic] one that I'm gonna do, but I'm just sort of getting [. . .] maybe something like an air hostess or something like that or cruise ship or something like that. Because it's, like travelling and getting more involved with people.

Patrick White: You want to travel then?

Student: Yeah, that's one of the main things I wanna do, is travel.

Patrick White: You mentioned [being] an air hostess or on a cruise ship. Is that just a vague idea at the moment?

Student: I used to be more sure when I was a bit younger that I wanted to actually be an air hostess. But as I've got older I've thought, well there's other things I could do. And I did actually get it checked up, the qualifications and stuff you need to be an air hostess or cruise ship assistant or something like that [. . .] They mentioned about glasses and stuff and how some [employers] are a bit dodgy about it. And I've been warned about that as well because I don't wear my glasses enough. And it just sort of gave me some idea.

[. . .]

Patrick White: It's not a very settled life, a lot of time in the air. You're not afraid of flying then? [laughs]

Student: No. [laughs] I'm not very good at travelling in a coach and stuff like that, but I'm not afraid of flying, no. I don't mind that.

Patrick White: What about on a cruise ship. You're not seasick?
Student: No, I'm not seasick. I'm not overly really confident on boats, but it's usually smaller ones that I'm not very good on.
[. . .]
Student: No. I don't really know what actually made me think [of it]. I think it was just things I'd watched on telly and just the fact that I've always liked [travelling]. I haven't travelled that much in my life, but it just interested me and I sort of clicked and that was it then, I just said that's the sort of thing I wanted to do.

The extract suggests that this student knows very little about what working on a cruise ship or as an air hostess actually involves. Her ideas appear to be based, at least partly, on what she had seen on television. More importantly, however, it demonstrates that some students hold misconceptions about, or are at least ignorant of, the demands of the occupations to which they aspire.

These issues are clearly important in terms of the analyses conducted in this chapter. Any patterns have been derived from data relating to only 29 cases, and are compared to the results of larger-scale studies in order to place them in some kind of historical context rather than to confirm or challenge previous findings. Indeed, most of the analyses in this chapter should be considered as exploratory in nature. The relationship between students future plans and their sex is examined first, before occupational aspirations are compared to their class backgrounds.

Intended destinations: sex and participation

Previous research in both compulsory (Arnot *et al.* 1999) and post-compulsory education (e.g. Banks *et al.* 1992; Bates and Riseborough 1993) has found that students' choices of subjects and courses, as well as their vocational plans, are strongly 'gendered' and tend to correspond with traditional patterns of participation in both education and the labour market.

However, there is evidence to suggest that this situation is changing, at least in some areas. For example, for some time now female students have made up more than half the intake of medical students in higher education, a profession previously dominated by men. Changes in the occupational structure over the last three decades, especially the decline of the male-dominated manufacturing industries, have meant that the kinds of job available to those leaving education and training today are significantly different from those that their parents were faced with (Roberts 1995).

The measure employed to gauge the extent to which the students' career intentions were 'gendered' was relatively unsophisticated. Both post-16 plans and more distant occupational goals were assessed in terms of whether they matched current trends in terms of participation in education or the labour market for a member of that sex (see Chapter 3). Because of the small size of the sample, the analysis was conducted at the 'case' level and included students who had only considered their immediate post-16 destinations.

The first stage of the analysis involved assessing whether post-16 intentions and/or occupational aspirations of students matched traditional patterns of participation. Those which contradicted these patterns were coded as 'un-gendered' and those which corresponded to them classified as 'gendered'. Where the post-16 intentions and occupational aspirations of a student were in conflict, cases were recorded as 'mixed'. Any responses which were problematic in terms of the analytic strategy were separated as unclassified. This included subject areas or occupations that are balanced in terms of the sex of the workforce, for example.

Examples are discussed below to illustrate how the analysis operated. *Kingfisher student male #2* and *Portland student female #1* were both conducted as 'un-gendered', as the former intended to take A-levels in languages and humanities subjects and then train to become a primary school teacher. Both the subjects he aimed to study, and especially the professional position he wished to take up, are more often pursued by females than males. *Portland student female #1* planned to take an Advanced GNVQ in business studies and then apply to enter the RAF Police. Again these are both areas traditionally dominated by men.

The students in the sample, however, were much more likely to express aspirations which were aligned to traditional patterns of participation for their sex. *Railroad student female #5*, for example, hoped to take an Advanced GNVQ in Health and Social Care and work as a carer in a nursing home. *Gordon Cole student male #1* aimed to study

A-levels in maths, physics and chemistry, before going into higher education and then working in science.

A few students' occupational aspirations were at odds with their proposed post-16 intentions, and so were coded as 'mixed'. Whilst *Gordon Cole student female #1* wanted to study Health and Social Care in Years 12 and 13, she planned to enter the police force directly following this, contrasting an initial female-dominated area of study with a male-dominated profession. A similar situation was evident in the choices of *Railroad student male #3*, who after taking maths and sports studies, intended to train as a primary school teacher.

As can be seen from Table 7.1, the vast majority of students' plans, for both their immediate post-16 and future occupational destinations, were congruent with traditionally gendered patterns of participation. Out of the 47 cases classified, just under three-quarters (34) of the students provided narratives in which both their post-16 and/or future work intentions corresponded with such patterns. Even if the 'unclassified' cases are included, bringing the sample up to its full size of 59, the students coded in the 'gendered' category still account for over half the participants in the study.

By comparison, only seven students' intentions contrasted with traditional patterns of participation and were thus coded as 'un-gendered'. Six students returned 'mixed' responses whereby their two intentions conflicted in terms of their congruence with such patterns. Even in combination these groups represent a minority of the categorised responses, suggesting that very few individuals planned on following trajectories contrasting with traditional patterns of participation. In terms of the 'gendered' nature of both the students' immediate post-16 destinations *and* their occupational aspirations,

Table 7.1 Post-16 intentions and occupational aspirations by gender and occupational class

Gendered		**Un-gendered**		**Mixed**		**Unclassified**	
34		**7**		**6**		**12**	
M	**F**	**M**	**F**	**M**	**F**	**M**	**F**
19	15	5	2	4	2	10	2

Total no. of students = 59, Male students = 38, Female students = 21.

traditional gender roles appear to continue to influence students' preferences.

Occupational aspirations and class background

Table 7.2 shows the extent to which students' occupational aspirations corresponded with their occupational class background measured using Erikson and Goldthorpe's (1993) classification. Students were categorised as belonging to one of three different groups according to whether their aspirations were upward, downward or stable.

As can be seen, the majority of students in the analysis (18/32) fall into the 'stable' category, meaning that if they successfully followed their preferred trajectory they would end up in the same occupational class as their parents. Ten students' aspirations were located in the occupational class above their parents' and 4 were in the class below. It would seem that, at least among those students who had any occupational aspirations, the majority of the young people interviewed had ambitions which were congruent with their parents' class.

Table 7.2 also provides a breakdown of the direction of students' occupational aspirations according to their class backgrounds. As the numbers are very small, it would be misleading to look for meaningful patterns in these data, and they are only included for information. It should be noted that those from 'service' class backgrounds cannot move any further 'up' the scale and those from 'working' class backgrounds cannot move 'downwards'. The figures in the corresponding cells (all zeros) reflect nothing more than this.

The students' occupational aspirations, and the implications for social mobility, were also disaggregated by sex but no obvious gender differences were found. It was interesting to note, however, that

Table 7.2 Occupational aspirations and social mobility

Upward			**Stable**			**Downward**		
10			**18**			**4**		
W	**I**	**S**	**W**	**I**	**S**	**W**	**I**	**S**
2	8	0	4	1	13	0	2	2

W = working class, I = intermediate class, S = service class.

many more male students (n = 22) than female (n = 5) reported having no particular occupational aspirations. It could be that female students are more conscientious with their career-planning, as they have been found to be with course work and examinations (see: Arnot *et al.* 1996, 1999; Gorard 2001b) and that female students are thus taking activities oriented to future events more seriously. However, this topic would have to be investigated further before any firm conclusions are to be drawn.

Choices and cumulative trajectories

A basic analysis of the links between the decisions made in the choice stages and young people's vocational aspirations has been documented in previous chapters. Choices that were influenced by motivations to pursue particular occupations or professions were distinguished from those relating to other goals or preference. Further analysis conducted at the level of type of occupation was beyond the scope of this study. What can be shown, however, through the use of selected cases, is how individual choices, whilst always leaving some scope for changes in direction, cumulatively add to the construction of a trajectory. Such trajectories may be guided by career goals but this is not always the case.

The two examples examined below were not chosen for their particular strength as evidence of the cumulative nature of trajectories or because they demonstrate the roles played by individual choice and social and cultural factors in determining the destinations of young people. They were selected because in certain respects they represent particularly contrasting choice histories but ones demonstrating common themes in the choice processes of the students in the sample.

Railroad student female #5

Railroad student female #5 lives in Dean and is from a working class background, her mother working is a newsagent and her father as an electrician. She has an elder brother who works as a welder and a younger sister attending the same school. It appears from her account that she is a low achiever, academically. At the time of interview she intended to stay on at Railroad School to take a GNVQ in health and social care and to re-take her GCSE maths, as she shared her teacher's belief that she would fail on her first attempt. On completing her post-16 course she planned to work as a carer in a nursing home for the elderly. Although she originally intended to pursue a different but related career, an examination of her past actions and present intentions illuminates how, through a combination of choice and circumstance, her trajectory was formed over time.

Her choices of Key Stage 4 courses, made in Year 9, were generally 'exclusive' in nature. Although 'exclusive' decision-making behaviour was more common this year than in Year 11, it was still relatively uncommon, with students tending to pick their favourite subjects before moving on to 'exclude' others. She chose to study a vocational course in Years 10 and 11, a Diploma in Vocational Education (DOVE), because she 'didn't wanna do art [laughs]. And I didn't wanna do PE either [laughs]'. This was the first decision that contributed to her future trajectory, as new vocational qualifications have tended to be viewed by both employers and other gatekeepers as of lower status than academic ones (Roberts 1995). However, it need not have necessarily affected her post-16 destination dramatically, either in terms of course or institution pursued at that level. Holding such a qualification would have only restricted entry to the two selective grammar schools in the area.

The decisions *Railroad student female #5* had taken in terms of her post-16 destinations further shaped her trajectory. She reports that she originally 'was gonna go to LumberTech to do a Health and Beauty course. But it was just the fact of me getting there in the mornings and getting back and everything'. Although she does not expand on her concerns regarding travel, it is a possibility that financial considerations were important. Her general attitude towards her career progression, however, suggests that inertia or even apathy may also have contributed to her actions. Either way, this represents another turning point in her career, resulting in her decision to take a GNVQ in Health and Social Care instead of a specialist vocational qualification in Health and Beauty.

Her decision may also have been affected by interaction with her peers. The following extract shows *Railroad student female #5's* response when asked about her post-18 intentions.

Patrick White: So, d'you think that you're going to go straight into work after 18, when you've finished your GNVQ?
Student: Mmm . . . I don't know. I haven't really thought about it. But I know I just wanna stay on at sixth form and maybe go [on] to college. But if I can get a job, where my friend's working, she said she could get me a job, I'll prob'ly do that.
Patrick White: Where does she work?
Student: In Tipton Old Peoples' Home.
Patrick White: Is that in Dean?
Student: Yeah.

Railroad student female #5's aspirations appear to have been affected by what Hodkinson *et al.* (1996, pp. 149–150) describe as 'perceptions of what might be available and what might be appropriate'. Both her occupational ambitions (Beautician and Carer) were congruent with her class background and gender (and so 'appropriate') but information of local employment opportunities (what was 'available') gained through transmission of knowledge via 'informal networks' were also influential in deciding her final destination. Information sources such as these have previously been shown to be very important in gaining a foothold in the opportunity structure (see: Willis 1977; Roberts 1995).

It appeared likely that *Railroad student female #5* would follow this course of action, perhaps gaining employment locally. In this way she will reproduce both her class and geographical location, as well as conforming to traditional patterns of gendered participation in the opportunity structure. This trajectory was by no means inevitable (and could still change) but the above discussion shows how a combination of both her structural location and her own agency led to the gradual construction of a vocational direction.

Kingfisher student male #7

Kingfisher student male #7 is a student at Kingfisher Grammar School. His mother is a nurse and his father manages a recycling firm, placing him in a 'service' class background. He has a younger brother who failed the entrance exam for Kingfisher, chose not to attend the local comprehensive (Railroad) and is now enrolled at another local school. The decision to attend a grammar school was initiated by

Kingfisher student male #7, who approached his parents with the idea. In the extract below, he recounts the scenario.

Patrick White: So, how come you decided to come here?
Student: Well, it's not a comprehensive School, you have to take an exam to pass . . . and I took the exam and I passed, and recently it's just what I've heard about the school that the good grades it's produced over the years . . . made me come here.
Partick White: And were your parents involved as well?
Student: Yes . . .
Patrick White: They wanted you to come here as well?
Student: Well, they were backing my decision.
Patrick White: So, was it your idea to sit the exam in the first place?
Student: Yes, yes.

His reasons for wanting to attend a grammar school are unclear, as some of his rationalisations appear only to have been made subsequent to his enrolment at Kingfisher ('and recently'). However, that such an option was considered by *Kingfisher student male #7* and supported by his parents are reflections, perhaps, of his socio-cultural background. Here, in his first major educational transition, the *interaction* of structural (and resulting cultural) factors with individual choice can be seen.

His subsequent decisions in Years 9 and 11 were all 'inclusive' in nature. They were based solely on enjoyment in Year 9 but directed by vocational aspirations in Year 11. He has harboured ambitions to work in the motor racing industry for some time but only in Year 10 did they coalesce into firm plans, when he arranged a work experience placement at an engineering firm. In the extract below he describes the formulation of this post-16 plans.

Patrick White: Right . . . so what do you see yourself doing next year?
Student: Well, hopefully staying on at Kingfisher School for A-levels . . . maybe physics and maths, and then entrance to university.
Patrick White: So you're looking at doing engineering at university?
Student: Hopefully.

Patrick White: And is that why you wanted physics and maths?
Student: Yes.
Patrick White: How did you find out that you needed them?
Student: I actually wrote away to Coventry University, 'cos I know they're quite big in Engineering. They wrote back saying what sort of qualifications were needed.
Patrick White: So, will you just take two or will you have a third one?
Student: Erm . . . I think we have to take three, yes.
Patrick White: That's the school . . .?
Student: School requirement, yes. I'm not sure what to do yet, I'm having discussions with a careers advisor.

Kingfisher student male #7's attendance at a grammar school continues to impact on his trajectory as, if he enrols in the sixth form, he is required to take at least three A-levels. In this way, a decision made five years earlier continues as an influence, demonstrating the 'cumulative' impact that some educational decisions can have in relation to career trajectories. The work experience placement he arranged was also important in deciding his post-16 intentions. The fact that he organised a placement relevant to his vocational interests, rather than the most convenient alternative, is significant in itself. This was not as common as would have been supposed, with a large minority of students opting for the latter option. He also used the time in the placement to conduct research into entry routes into engineering.

Patrick White: And was [the work experience placement] good?
Student: Excellent, yes. Really good experience.
Patrick White: How long is that . . . a week?
Student: A week, yes.
Patrick White: Did that confirm your ideas about going into engineering?
Student: It certainly did.
Patrick White: And did you pick up any useful information about how to get into engineering?
Student: Yes. A lot of people I was talking to, they've done modern apprenticeships. But I was talking to one of the chiefs there and he said the best way now is

to go into further education and work your way from university.

Patrick White: So is that what you're aiming to do now?

Student: Yes.

Kingfisher student male #7's experience on the placement confirmed his intentions to enter engineering. He also used the placement as an opportunity to discuss entry routes into the occupation with employees at the firm. He liaised with workers at all levels of the company and as a result, having approached 'one of the chiefs', gained valuable information into the most propitious entry route to pursue.

Considering his (service class) background and current patterns of educational participation in the United Kingdom, it was likely that *Kingfisher student male #7* would have entered higher education regardless of his placement experience. What the example above demonstrates, however, is his pro-active use of 'networking' skills. It could be the case that an individual with similar aspirations but with different social and cultural experiences, may not have accessed the same information. Again, there is the possibility of choices interacting with, or being affected by the background of the individual who makes them.

It should be noted, however, that the kind of networking skills displayed by this student may not be very different from the scouting of local labour market opportunities conducted by *Railroad student female #5*. The most important difference may be the nature of the networks to which the two students gained access, rather than any difference in terms of their ability or willingness to engage in this type of activity.

The final example of the formation of this young person's trajectory is linked with his future plans to enter higher education. Perhaps because of the economic situation of his parents, he appears to assume unquestioningly that entering higher education will be an option. Other students may not be planning so far ahead because of their uncertainty of the degree of financial support their parents will be able to offer them. Some choices are directly dependent on young people's socio-economic background and, perhaps, their 'financial cultures', including attitudes towards borrowing (Hesketh 1999). The degree to which *Kingfisher student male #7* is planning his educational future is demonstrated by the accounts he gives of the research he has already conducted into potential higher education destinations.

As with the example of *Railroad student female #5*, it is possible to see the gradual construction of *Kingfisher student male #7's* career trajectory, influenced both by his socio-economic and cultural background, and the decisions he has made over time. His trajectory, although leading to a more flexible portfolio of experiences and qualifications, has been influenced from as far back as his decision to attend Kingfisher school.

Rees *et al.* (1997, p. 487) argue that 'learning behaviour is conceived as the product of individual calculation and active choice, but within the parameters set by both access to learning opportunities and collective norms'. Hodkinson *et al.* (1996, pp. 149–150) make a similar observation that

> young people make career decisions within their horizons for action, which incorporate externally located opportunities in the labour market . . . Perceptions of what might by available and what might be appropriate influence decisions, so that opportunities are simultaneously subjective and objective.

The two cases examined above exemplify the ideas set out by both these groups of researchers.

Summary

Students' choices of post-16 destinations matched traditional (and more recent) patterns of participation in terms of occupational class background and gender. Their occupational aspirations were also congruent with recent trends in labour market entry. With respect to both immediate post-16 destinations and occupational aspirations, this may be explicable in terms of students' individual attainment levels, which are closely related to class backgrounds. However, gender differences cannot be explained so easily, as any differences are much smaller.

This chapter showed how students begin to construct their trajectories very early in their educational careers, perhaps with their choice of secondary school. The choices students face in each educational choice year are shaped by those made in all previous choice years. A 'cumulative trajectory' is thus constructed that can, in certain ways, determine the scope of choices made at each subsequent choice stage in an individual's career.

In the final chapter, the findings from the study are summarised and important themes are highlighted. The state of current research in the area is considered, and possible implications for policy and practice are addressed.

8
Concluding Remarks

This final chapter is divided into four sections. In the first section, the 'state of the art' of research into post-16 choice is considered, alongside recommendations for improving the quality of work in the area. The second section briefly summarises findings in the area that have been consistently documented by independent studies. The contribution of this study assessed in relation to these two discussions is then considered, before implications for policy and practice are explored.

The 'state of the art' of research into post-16 choice

As has been demonstrated in this book, much can be learned about post-16 transitions using only existing, publicly available data. Data collected by the DfES or as part of the YCS can provide valuable insights into the experiences of young people approaching the end of their compulsory schooling. At the very least, national and regional data sets can set the context within which studies take place.

Few studies, however, make use of these resources. Notable exceptions included work by Cheng (1995) and Payne (2001a, b) whose multivariate analyses of YCS data have provided some of the most valuable and robust findings in the area. As Gorard (2003) has noted, however, analysis of existing data set need not be complicated nor time-consuming. It is particularly valuable in the case of small-scale studies, as it allows research findings to be located within a wider context, benefiting both researchers and readers. At present, however, using data in this way is relatively uncommon.

As Payne (2003) notes, longitudinal research in the area is still relatively scarce, and typically restricted to small-scale studies. The analyses of YCS data provide another noticeable exception to this although, as discussed in Chapter 2, these data are not without their problems. Perhaps it is time for a large-scale longitudinal study using a variety of methods of data collection and analysis.

A particular concern is that many researchers appear to be 'wedded' to particular theoretical approaches and concepts. The work of Pierre Bourdieu is often cited by researchers in the area but it is less clear how this has contributed to our understanding. Indeed, as Sjöberg (2005) has noted, attachments to particular theories often lead to stagnation rather than progress.

Several studies have purported to document the 'process' of decision making but few of these have done so satisfactorily. When examined closely, some models appear to be static in nature, and often include problematic theoretical constructs. It is hoped that the present study will be considered to have made modest progress in this area.

Our current knowledge

The context of post-16 choice

Since the mid-1990s, young people have approached the end of compulsory schooling in an environment in which the vast majority of their peers will continue their education after Year 11, most studying or training on a full-time basis. A large minority of these will enter higher education. In fact, almost all those who have the necessary minimum qualifications will do so.

Students' post-16 education takes place in a national context of high, and improving, pass rates. Academic success, however, continues to be differentiated by social and occupational class background, although the mechanisms by which this operates remain unclear. While there is a small difference in the attainment of males and females, there is a much larger difference in the subject areas they pursue, which tend to reflect traditional patterns of participation.

Choices and influences

Decisions relating to institutions are sometimes restricted by the availability of specialist courses but such courses are pursued by only a minority of students. For students interested in less specialised qualifications or subject areas, however, the 'reputation' of an institution may be more influential. There are also links between levels of attainment and the type of post-16 institutions attended, and a tendency for students to remain at their present institution even if this means compromising on course choice.

Subject areas are most commonly chosen for reasons relating to enjoyment but occasionally related to vocational ambitions. They continue to follow the traditional patterns of participation of each sex, however. Qualification choice is limited by previous attainment, influenced slightly by gender, but is likely to relate to intentions regarding entry to either the labour market or HE.

While traditionally occupational aspirations have been central to the study of post-16 choice, at the turn of the millennium they do not impact greatly on the choices made by students in Year 11. Perhaps because of the extended transition between school and work, most students do not have concrete ideas about their occupational futures by the end of their compulsory schooling.

Parents and other family members continue to be the most influential sources of information and advice. Young people are much more likely to seek guidance from family members than 'formal' sources such as careers professionals. It would appear that, at least from the perspective of students, CEG plays only a marginal role in their decision making.

The status of the information drawn on by parents, however, is questionable. The present study found evidence to suggest that both parents and students often held very strong beliefs about the 'transformative capacities' of educational institutions. It was commonly suggested that the particular institution attended could impact dramatically on the performance of a student. Although this is clearly a possibility, existing research on 'school effects' suggests this would be very unlikely.

The contribution of this study

As this study was limited in terms of time and other resources, its contribution to the area is inevitably modest. It has, however, developed a model of decision making that has a genuine capacity to capture an element of 'process'. The cross-sectional, rather than longitudinal, nature of the research has placed limitations on longer-term development of the phenomenon but, as all studies must necessarily rely on young people's accounts for data in this area, this is not a critical weakness.

The choice 'types', 'stages' and 'models' developed in this book are intended to serve as 'heuristic devices' rather than definitive descriptions of decision making. It is hoped that they provide, at the very least, a starting point for the development of more sophisticated and robust concepts and constructs.

Because of the relatively small size of the sample, any analysis of the impact of class or sex on decision making was necessarily exploratory. The temptation to make wide-ranging generalisations, based on only a handful of cases, was resisted. Unfortunately, many studies with even smaller samples have not been so restrained.

Some patterns in the data, however, were certainly noteworthy. As there were a much larger number of choices than there were students, robust patterns among individual decisions were much easier to identify. There were strong links between particular 'factors' and 'rationales', and students appeared to make decisions in a certain sequence. The importance of previous choices in shaping future trajectories was demonstrated, and it was seen that decisions made as early as Year 6 could influence post-16 destinations.

Policy and practical implications

There have been three recent government publications that address issues relating to this area of study (DfES 2004, 2005, 2006). It has been made quite clear that the government views current levels of post-16 participation as 'scandalously low' (DfES 2006, p. 3) and intends to implement initiatives to increase them. It has also announced intentions to increase the range of choices faced by 14–19 year-olds (DfES 2005, 2006), especially with respect to combining vocational and academic options. Greater collaboration between schools and colleges in providing education and training for 14–16 year-olds has also been viewed as desirable (DfES 2004, 2006).

Should these changes introduce a real element of increased choice for young people, there may well be some benefits. Choices in Year 9, for example, are often very restricted and led to some young people in this study making choices by excluding undesirable subjects rather than choosing between alternatives that they enjoyed. However, young people at the end of compulsory schooling already face a very wide range of possible routes, with a huge number of possible combinations of subject areas, qualifications and institutional types. The advantage of increased choice at this transition will be dependent, to a great extent, on the ability of choosers to successfully negotiate the decision-making process.

It appears that most young people actively engage with the post-16 decision-making process. What is also clear, however, is that they tend to rely on their family for advice and support, and make little use of formal career education and guidance (CEG) services. It is also the case that some students, quite understandably given their age and experience, hold very naïve views about the careers to which they aspire and the value or utility of particular subject areas or qualifications.

While the Tomlinson report (DfES 2004, p. 6) highlighted the need for 'guidance in making choices about further learning and careers', the two White Papers produced subsequently (DfES 2005, 2006) do not make this a central theme in their calls for reform. Whether or not students are faced with increased choice, it is essential that they both have access to good quality CEG provision. It is equally important that they *value* this guidance and make use of it during their decision making. Given the findings in this and other studies, this may be no easy task. It should be a matter of central concern to policymakers in the area, however, and is noticeably underemphasised in recent publications.

Final remarks

It is hoped that the research documented in this book is useful not only to academic researchers but also to practitioners and policymakers. While no single piece of research can provide definitive answers to long-standing questions, this study provides an original and innovative contribution to the study of post-16 choice. It should be remembered, however, that policy and practice decisions are necessarily based as much on value judgements as they are on empirical evidence. Research can provide an account of how young people make educational and career decisions, and it can highlight issues that have previously been ignored or gone unnoticed, but it cannot be expected to deliver directives on the future of education.

Appendix

This appendix contains detailed information on the geographical area in which the fieldwork took place, the educational institutions involved, and the composition of the student sample. It has been appended to the main text to minimise disruption to the structure of the report.

The presentation of data is accompanied by a brief discussion of the possible implication of the socio-demographic context in which the fieldwork took place. However, sufficient information is provided to enable readers to make independent judgements about how social, economic and institutional factors may have impacted on the narratives provided by the young people interviewed.

The Local authority areas of Dean and Green Valley

The towns of Dean and Davchester are just 15 miles apart but lie in different local authorities (LAs). While Dean is located in the local authority of the same name, Davchester is part of the Green Valley LA. Both towns, however, fall within Lumbertonshire local education authority (LEA).

Income and employment

As can be seen in Table A1, in terms of income and employment, both LAs are relatively prosperous. While Dean is just outside the top third of LAs on both indices, Green Valley is in the top 8 per cent of LAs in terms of employment and the top 12 per cent in terms of income. In 2001, only 1.7 per cent of Green Valley's economically active adults aged between 16 and 74 were unemployed. In the same year the figure for Dean was slightly higher, at 2.4 per cent (National Statistics 2005).

Given the low rates of unemployment in the two LAs, it is unsurprising that only a small proportion of the population claim Job Seekers Allowance (JSA) in both Dean and Green Valley. In Dean the rate was less than half of the average for England and Wales, and in Green Valley it was below one-third of

Table A1 Indices of income and employment,* by Local Authority, 2004

	Dean	**Green Valley**
Rank of income scale	235	313
Rank of employment scale	226	329

* Ranking of 354 Local Authorities, with highest ranking equating to lowest income and lowest levels of employment.
Source: ONS (2006).

Table A2 Income-based job seekers allowance claimants as percentage of population, August 2003

	Dean	**Green Valley**	**South West**	**England and Wales**
JSA claimants (%)	0.5	0.3	0.6	1.1

Source: ONS (2006).

the national rate. Both LAs had rates below the average for the South West region (Table A2).

The social and economic characteristics of the region where the study took place should not be ignored in any study. As Payne (2003, p. 49) notes, evidence indicates that 'young people's choices at 16 are shaped partly by the opportunities they see in the local labour market, including both the industrial structure and the level of demand for labour'.

Given the prosperity of both Dean and Green Valley, it might be expected that the young people in the present study would be relatively optimistic about their labour market futures, both in terms of their chances of gaining employment and the status and income of the occupations they would work in. This, in turn, could affect the kind of decisions they make at the end of compulsory schooling.

Education

While both Dean and Green Valley had higher average income levels and lower rates of unemployment compared to the South West region, and England and Wales as a whole, the qualification levels of adults in both LAs are much closer to the regional and national averages. In 2001, the proportion of adults with no formal qualifications in both LAs was very similar, at around 23 per cent, only a few percentage points lower than the regional rate, and approximately 80 per cent of the national average. There were also proportionally more adults with qualifications equivalent to NVQ levels 4 or 5 compared to the regional and national aggregates but, again, these differences were not nearly as large as the economic disparities discussed earlier (see Table A3).

Table A3 Qualification levels of resident population aged 16–74, April 2001 (%)

	Dean	Green Valley	South West	England and Wales
No qualifications(%)	23.6	23.3	26.2	29.1
Level 4/5 (%)	22.9	24.0	18.8	19.8

Level 4/5 includes First degree; Higher degree; NVQ levels 4 and 5; HNC; HND; Qualified Teacher Status; Qualified Medical Doctor; Qualified Dentist; Qualified Nurse; Midwife; Health Visitor.

Source: National Statistics (2005).

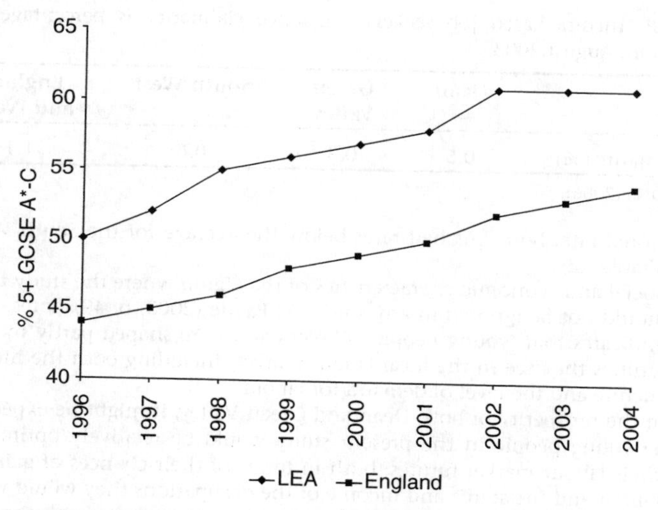

Figure A1 Pupils achieving five or more GCSE A*–C grades, Lumbertonshire LEA and England, 1996–2004.

Source: DfES (1995–2006).

The GCSE results of school pupils in Lumbertonshire LEA, within which Dean and Green Valley are located, have been consistently above the national average for at least a decade. As can be seen in Figure A1, a greater proportion of students in Lumbertonshire LEA finished compulsory schooling with five or more GCSEs at grade C or above, compared to the national average, with Lumbertonshire students at least 7 percentage points ahead. In 1998, the year in which the students in the study took their GCSEs, the difference was eight percentage points, or nearly 17 per cent.

As the relationship between parental occupation and children's academic attainment has been well established (see Chapters 1 and 3) it is perhaps unsurprising that students in Lumbertonshire LEA attain better GCSE results, on average, than students aggregated at a national level. However, as discussed in the previous chapter, the 'benchmark' figure of five or more passes at grade C or above is only one measure of attainment in this area. The proportion of students failing to gain any passes may be more important in terms of the consequences for future labour market success.

Considering their relative advantage in terms of educational attainment, it would be expected that the post-16 routes taken by the students in Dean and Green Valley would tend towards higher status destinations. If national trends apply to the students in the present study, and they may not, their higher levels of attainment would lead to a larger than average proportion considering academic rather than vocational qualifications, and a greater number aspiring to enter higher education.

Ethnicity

Ethnically, the South West region is extremely homogeneous, with nearly 98 per cent of the population registering as 'White' in the 2001 Census. Green Valley and Dean have an even smaller proportion of residents from minority ethnic groups, at just over 1 per cent of the populace.

As has already been highlighted, none of the 59 students in the sample reported having ethnic minority origins, and so the topic of ethnicity could not be investigated in the present study. Given the data in Table A4, it is unlikely that many of the sample had regular contact with members of minority ethnic groups at all.

Summary

As the data presented above demonstrate, the geographic area in which the fieldwork took place is relatively affluent. The residents of Green Valley have very high levels of income and unemployment in the LA is very low. Dean is not quite as well off in either respect, but is still among the most affluent areas of the United Kingdom. The populations of both LAs tend to be slightly better educated than the national average and, as a group, secondary school pupils in Lumbertonshire LEA consistently get higher than average GCSE results. There are very few members of minority ethnic groups in either LA, and this is reflected in the sample of students, all of whom were ethnically 'White'.

Table A4 Distribution of ethnic groups (%), by local authority and region, 2001

	Dean %	Green Valley %	South West %	England and Wales %
White	98.7	98.8	97.7	91.3
All minority ethnic groups	1.3	1.2	2.3	8.7

Source: National Statistics (2005).

Table A5 Characteristics of schools in the sample, 1997/98

Name	Type	Location	Age range	Roll	5+ GCSE A*–C (%)	5+ GCSE A*–C (%)	A-Level points*
Gordon Cole	GM	Sparkwood	11–18	792	54	55	18.6
Kingfisher	Grammar	Dean	11–18	808	89	94	19.4
Meadow Lane	Comp.	Davchester	11–16	1061	64	69	n/a
Portland	Comp.	Danford	11–18	841	64	61	17.5
Railroad	Comp.	Dean	11–18	967	41	43	12.9
Redpost	Comp.	Davchester	11–16	714	63	68	n/a

* Average points score for students taking two or more A–levels.

Source: DfES.

Railroad

Railroad School is a mixed–sex comprehensive school taking students from 11 to 18 years. In 1997/98 it had 967 students on the school role, including 168 sixth formers. It is the only comprehensive school in Dean and careers staff reported that its reputation in the town suffered because of its former status as a secondary modern school. Indeed, in terms of performance in GCSE examinations, its students were the least successful of all six institutions in the study (see Figure A2). The average A-level point score for students taking two or more A-levels was 12.9.

Meadow Lane

Meadow Lane School is one of two comprehensives in Davchester, both taking students from 11 to 16 years. In 1997/98, 1061 students were enrolled at the school. Meadow Lane has a similar profile of GCSE results to both Portland and Redpost.

Redpost School

Redpost School is the other comprehensive in Davchester and, like Meadow Lane, has no sixth form. In 2001, 714 students were on the school roll. As can be seen in Figure A2, historical trends in GCSE performance has been similar to Portland but consistently slightly below those at Meadow Lane, the only other state secondary school in Davchester.

Portland

Portland School is, alongside Railroad, one of only two comprehensive schools in the study that takes students from ages 11 to 18. It is located in Danford, eight miles from Davchester, and had 841 students on the school roll in 1997/98. Portland students' performance in GCSE exams has been close to that of those at Meadow Lane. Whilst in the mid-1990s Portland students

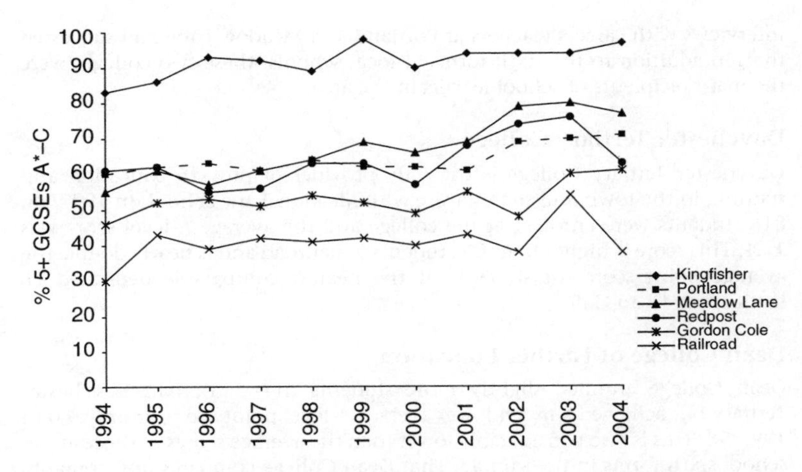

Figure A2 Pupils achieving five or more GCSEs at A*–C, by school, 1994–2004.
Source: DfES (1995–2006).

had outperformed those at Meadow Lane, since 1999 the latter institution has produced consistently better results. In 1997/98, 152 students were in the sixth form and the average A-level score was 17.5 points.

Kingfisher

Kingfisher School is the only grammar school in the sample. It is also the only single-sex school and is located opposite a girls' grammar school in Dean. In 1997/98, 880 students were on the school roll, 200 of whom were in the sixth form. As the only selective school, it is perhaps unsurprising that its students perform better in GCSE examinations than those at the other, non-selective, institutions in the sample. As can be seen in Figure A2, the gap in performance between Kingfisher and Meadow Lane is considerable. The average A/AS-level point score per pupil was 19.4 in 1997/98.

Gordon Cole

Gordon Cole School is located in Sparkwood, a small town 12 miles from Davchester. It had originally been a grammar school but in 1998, when the fieldwork was conducted, was the only institution in the sample to hold grant-maintained status. It takes students from 11–18 and in 1997/98 had 792 students on the school roll. In terms of performance in GCSE exams, Gordon Cole outperforms only Railroad, with all other schools in the sample scoring higher according to the standard benchmark. In 2001 there were 130 students in the sixth form and the average A-level point score per pupil was 18.6.

In addition to the fieldwork based at the above institutions, interviews with staff were also conducted at two local further education institutions. Pilot interviews with careers teachers at Portland and Meadow Lane had suggested that, in addition to the sixth forms at local schools, these two colleges were the main recipients of school leavers in the area.

Davchester Tertiary College

Davchester Tertiary College is the only provider of post–16 education and training in the town and shares a site with Meadow Lane School. In 1997/98, 816 students were enrolled at the college and the average A-level score was 17.1. This score is higher than for students at Railroad and is nearly double the average point score for students at the nearest comparable dedicated FE institution, Dean College.

Dean College of Further Education

Dean College enrolled slightly more students (n = 933) than Davchester Tertiary but achieved a much lower average A-level point score, at only 9.6 in 1997/98. This is also considerably lower than the average scores of those at the school sixth forms in the sample. That Dean College compares unfavourably with school sixth forms in terms of academic outcomes is unsurprising, given the traditionally more diverse student intake associated with further education institutions. Given the very high average point score of students at Davchester Tertiary, who outperform the majority of those at school sixth forms, it might be expected that other post-16 institutions, such as Dean College, would be unlikely to compete in academic terms.

The resulting sample composition is shown in Table A6, broken down by both sex and occupational class background (using Erikson and Goldthorpe's (1993) CASMIN scheme). Where students had two working parents, the highest ranked occupation was used to classify their background. Given the economic and labour market profile of the area, it is not surprising that nearly half of the respondents came from service class backgrounds. A significant minority (20/59) of the students had parents from intermediate class backgrounds, whilst only nine were from working class families.

Student Sample

The sample, while not large, is relatively diverse in terms of sex and occupational class. As has already been noted, a sample of this size could never be representative of the national (or even local) student population, and the sample is inevitably an artefact of both the selection procedure and the intake of the schools that participated in the study. Being explicit about the selection of the sample, its resulting characteristics, and the implications for any conclusions drawn, however, allows judgements to be made regarding the scope for the generalisation of any findings.

Table A6 Composition of sample by occupational class and sex

	Working	Intermediate	Service	Unknown	Total
Male	6	13	18	1	38
Female	3	7	10	1	21
Total	9	20	28	2	59

Bibliography

Adey, K. and Biddulph, M. (2001) 'The influence of pupil perceptions on subject choice at 14+ in geography and history', *Education Studies*, 27 (4): 439–450.

Aggleton, P. (1987) *Rebels without a Cause? Middle Class Youth and the Transition from School to Work*. Lewes: Falmer Press.

Andres, L., Ainsef, P., Krahn, H., Looker, D. and Thiessen, L. (1999) 'The persistence of social structure: cohort, class and gender effects on the occupational aspirations and expectations of Canadian youth', *Journal of Youth Studies*, 2 (3): 261–282.

Arnot, M., David, M. and Weiner, G. (1996) *Educational Reform and Gender Equality in Schools*. Manchester: Equal Opportunites Commision

Arnot, M., David, M. and Weiner, G. (1999) *Closing the Gender Gap : Post-war Education and Social Change*. Cambridge: Blackwell Publishers.

Ashton, D. N. and Field, D. (1976) *Young Workers*. London: Hutchingson.

Ashton, D. N., Maguire, M. J. and Spilsbury, M. (1990) *Restructuring the Labour Market: The Implications for Youth*. Basingstoke: Macmillan.

Bagley, C., Woods, P. A. and Glatter, R. (2001) 'Rejecting schools: Towards a fuller understanding of the process of parental choice', *School Leadership & Management*, 21 (3): 309–325.

Ball, S., Maguire, M. and Macrae, S. (2000) *Choice, Pathways and Transitions Post-16: New Youth, New Economies in the Global City*. London: Routledge.

Banks, M., Bates, I., Breakwell, G., Bynner, J., Emler, N., Jamieson, L. and Roberts, K. (1992) *Careers and Identities*. Milton Keynes: Open University Press.

Bates, I. (1990) 'The politics of careers education and guidance: a case for scrutiny', *British Journal of Guidance and Counselling*, 18 (1): 66–83.

Bates I. and Riseborough, G. (1993) *Careers and Identities*. Milton Keynes: Open University Press.

Bell, J. F., Malacova, E. and Shannon, M. (2005) 'The changing pattern of A-level/AS uptake in England', *Curriculum Journal*, 16 (3): 391–400.

Biggart, A., Deacon, K., Dobbie, F., Furlong, A., Given, L. and Hinds, K. (2004) *Findings from the Scottish School Leavers Survey: 17 in 2003*. Edinburgh: Scottish

Executive. IBSN 0755938674. Available at: http://www. scotland.gov.uk/library5/education/17in03.pdf

Blackburn, R. (2003) 'The concept of capital: sense and nonsense', paper presented to SSRG Conference, Cardiff 2003.

Bloomer, M. and Hodkinson, P. (2000) 'Learning careers: continuity and change in young people's dispositions to learning', *British Educational Research Journal*, 26 (5): 583–597.

Bourdieu, P. (1986) 'The forms of capital', in J.G. Richardson (Ed.), *Handbook of Theory and Research for the Sociology of Education*. New York: Greenwood Press.

Bourdieu, P. and Passeron, J.-C. (1977) *Reproduction in Education, Society and Culture*. London: Sage.

Bowles, S. and Gintis, H. (1976) *Schooling in Capitalist America: Educational Reform and the Contradictions of Economic Life*. London: Routledge and Kegan Paul.

Brooks, R. (2003) 'Discussing higher education choices: differences and difficulties', *Research Papers in Education*, 18 (3): 237–258.

Brooks, R. (2004) ' "My mum would be as pleased as punch if I actually went, but my dad seems a bit more particular about it": parental involvement in young people's higher education choices', *British Educational Research Journal*, 30 (4): 495–514.

Brown, P. (1987) *Schooling Ordinary Kids*. London: Tavistock.

Bryman, A. (1988) *Quality and Quantity in Social Research*. London: Unwin Hyman.

Bynner, J. and Roberts, K. (Eds) (1991) *Youth and Work: Transition to Employment in England and Germany*. London: Anglo German Foundation.

Carter, M. P. (1962) *Home, School and Work: A Study of the Education and Employment of Young People in Britain*. London: Pergamon.

Cheng, Y. (1995) *Staying On in Full-Time Education after Sixteen: Do Schools Make a Difference?*, Youth Cohort Study Paper No. 37. London: Employment Department.

Cleaves, A. (2005) 'The formation of science choices in secondary schools', *International Journal of Science Education*, 26 (5): 613–625.

Coffey, A. and Atkinson, P. (1996) *Making Sense of Qualitative Data: Complementary Research Strategies*. London: Sage.

Collins, H. and Pinch, T. (1998) *The Golem: What You Should Know about Science*. [2nd edn.]. Cambridge: Canto.

Courtney, G. and Mekkelholt, P. (1996) *England and Wales Youth Cohort Study Handbook: The First Ten Years*. London: HMSO.

David, M., West, A. and Ribbens, J. (1994) *Mother's Intuition? Choosing Secondary Schools*. East Sussex: Falmer Press.

Delamont, S. (2000) 'The anomalous beasts: hooligans and the sociology of education', *Sociology*, 34 (1): 95–111.

Dey, I. (1995) 'Reducing fragmentation in qualitative research', in U. Kelle (Ed.). *Computer-Aided Qualitative Data Analysis: Theory, Method and Practice*. London: Sage.

DfES (1995–2006) *Research and Statistics Gateway*. [on-line]. London: DfES. Available from: http://www.dfes.gov.uk/rsgateway/

DfES (2003a) 'Review of the initial entry rate into higher education', *National Statistics Quality Review Series, No. 24*. London: DfES.
DfES (2003b) *Widening Participation in Higher Education*. London: DfES.
DfES (2004) *14–19 Curriculum and Qualifications Reform: Final Report of the Working Group on 14–19 Reform*. Nottingham: DfES. http://www.dfes.gov.uk/14–19/documents/Final%20Report.pdf
DfES (2005) *14–19 Education and Skills Summary*. Nottingham: DfES. http://www.dfes.gov.uk/14–19/documents/14–19whitepapersum.pdf
DfES (2006) *Further Education: Raising Skills, Improving Life Chances*. Nottingham: DfES. http://www.dfes.gov.uk/publications/furthereducation/docs/6608-FE%20WP%20Summ.pdf
Dolton, P., Makepeace, G., Hutton, S. and Audas, R. (1999) *Making the Grade: Education, the Labour Market and Young People*. York: Joseph Rowntree Foundation.
Echols, F. and Willms, J. (1995) 'Reasons for school choice in Scotland', *Journal of Education Policy*, 5 (3): 207–222.
Eiser, J. and van der Plight, J. (1988) *Attitudes and Decisions*. London: Routledge.
Erikson, R. and Goldthorpe, J. H. (1993) *The Constant Flux: A Study of Class Mobility in Industrial Societies*. Oxford: Clarendon Press.
Evans, K. and Furlong, A. (1997) 'Metaphors of youth transitions: niches, pathways, trajectories or navigations', in J. Bynner, L. Chisolm and A. Furlong (Eds), *Youth, Citizenship and Social Change in a European Context*. London: Ashgate.
Fitz-Gibbon, C. (1997) 'Listening to students and the 50% framework', in T. Edwards, C. Fitz-Gibbon, F. Hardman, R. Haywood and N. Meager (Eds), *Separate but Equal? A Levels and GNVQs*. London: Routledge.
Fitz-Gibbon, C. (1999) 'Long-term consequences of curriculum choices with particular reference to mathematics and science', *School Effectiveness and School Improvement*, 10 (2): 217–232.
Foskett, N. H. and Hemsley-Brown, J. (2001) *Choosing Futures: Young people's Decision-Making in Education, Training and Career Markets*. London: RoutledgeFalmer.
Foskett, N. H. and Hesketh, A. J. (1997) 'Constructing choice in contiguous and parallel markets: institutional and school leavers' responses to the new educational marketplace', *Oxford Review of Education*, 23 (3): 299–319.
Furlong, A. (1992) *Growing Up in a Classless Society?* Edinburgh: Edinburgh University Press.
Furlong, A. (1993) *Schooling for Jobs: Changes in the Career Preparation of British Secondary School Children*. Adershot: Avebury.
Furlong, A. (2005) 'Cultural dimensions of decisions about educational participation among 14- to 19-year-olds: the parts that Tomlinson doesn't reach', *Journal of Education Policy*, 20 (3): 379–389.
Furlong, A. and Biggart, A. (1999) 'Framing "choices": a longitudinal study of occupational aspirations among 13- to 16-year-olds', *Journal of Education and Work*, 12 (1): 21–35.
Furlong, A. and Cartmell, F. (1995) 'Aspirations and opportunity structure: 13 year-olds in areas with restricted opportunities', *British Journal of Guidance and Counselling*, 23 (3): 361–375.

Furlong, A. and Cartmell, F. (1997) *Young People and Social Change: Individualisation and Risk in Late Modernity*. Buckingham: Open University Press.

Gewirtz, S., Ball, S. J. and Bowe, R. (1995) *Markets, Choice and Equity in Education*. Buckingham: Open University Press.

Gillborn, D. and Youdell, D. (1999) *Rationing Education: Policy, Practice, Reform and Equity*. Buckingham: Open University Press.

Ginzberg, E., Ginzberg, S. W., Axelrad, S. and Herma, J. L. (1951) *Occupational Choice*. New York: Columbia University Press.

Goldthorpe, J. H. (1996) 'Class analysis and the reorientation of class theory: the case of persisting differentials in educational attainment', *British Journal of Sociology*, 47 (3): 481–505.

Gorard, S. (1997) *School Choice in an Established Market*. Aldershot: Ashgate.

Gorard, S. (1999) 'Keeping a sense of proportion: the "politician's error" in analysing school outcomes', *British Journal of Educational Studies*, 47 (3): 235–246.

Gorard, S. (2000) *Education and Social Justice*. Cardiff: University of Wales Press.

Gorard, S. (2001a) *Quantitative Methods in Educational Research: The Role of Numbers Made Easy*. London: Continuum.

Gorard, S. (2001b) 'An alternative account of "boys underachievement at school" ', *Welsh Journal of Education*, 10 (2): 4–14.

Gorard, S. (2002) 'Curiosity and surprise: the twin pillars of research', Birmingham University Student Conference Plenary, June 2002.

Gorard, S. (2003) *Combining Methods in Educational and Social Research*. London: Continuum.

Gorard, S. (2004) *Combining Methods in Educational and Social Research*. Maidenhead: Open University Press.

Gorard, S., Rees, G., Fevre, R. and Furlong, J. (1998) 'Learning trajectories: travelling towards a learning society?', *International Journal of Lifelong Education*, 17 (6): 400–410.

Gorard, S., Rees, G. and Salisbury, J. (2001) 'The differential attainment of boys and girls at school: investigating the patterns and their determinants', *British Educational Research Journal*, 27 (2): 125–139.

Gorard, S. and Smith, E. (2004) 'What is "underachievement" at school?', *School Leadership and Management*, 24 (2): 205–225.

Gorard, S. and Taylor, C. (2001) 'Student funding and hardship in Wales: a statistical summary', *Report to the National Assembly Investigation Group on Student Hardship*. Cardiff: National Assembly for Wales. ISBN 0750426853.

Gottfredson, L. S. (1981) 'Circumscription and compromise: a developmental theory of occupational aspirations', *Journal of Counselling Psychology*, 28: 545–579.

Gray, J., Jesson, D., and Sime, N. (1992) 'The "discouraged worker" revisited: post-16 participation in education south of the border', *Sociology*, 26: 493–505.

Halsey, A. H., Heath, A. F. and Ridge, J. M. (1980) *Origins and Destinations: Family, Class and Education in Modern Britain*. Oxford: Clarendon.

Hammersley, M. and Atkinson, P. (1995) *Ethnography: Principles in Practice*. (2nd edn). London: Routledge.

Harris, S. (1992a) 'Careers teachers: who are they and what do they do?', *British Journal of Sociology of Education*, 7 (3): 337–357.

Harris, S. (1992b) 'A career on the margins? The position of careers teachers in schools', *British Journal of Sociology of Education*, 13 (2): 163–176.

Heath, R. (2002) *Language, Culture and Markets in Further Education*. Unpublished PhD thesis. Cardiff. University of Wales.

Heath, R. (2002) *Language, Culture and Markets in Further Education*. Unpublished PhD thesis. Cardiff University: School of Social Sciences.

Hemsley-Brown, J. (1999) 'College Choice: perceptions and priorities', *Educational Management and Administration*, 27 (1): 85–98.

Hesketh, A. J. (1999) 'Towards an economic sociology of the student financial experience of higher education', *Journal of Education Policy*, 14 (4): 385–410.

Hodkinson, P. (1995) 'How young people make career decisions', *Education and Training*, 37 (8): 3–8.

Hodkinson, P., Sparkes, A. and Hodkinson, H. (1996) *Triumphs and Tears: Young People, Markets and the Transition from School to Work*. London: David Fulton.

Keys, M. and Maychell, K. with Evans, C., Brooks, R., Lee, B. and Pathak, S. (1998) *Staying On: A Study of Young People's Decisions about School Sixth Forms, Sixth-Form Colleges and Colleges of Future Education*. Berkshire: NFER.

Kidd, J. M., and Wardman, M. (1999) 'Post-16 course choice: a challenge for guidance', *British Journal of Guidance and Counselling*, 27 (2): 259–274.

Lawrence, D. (1992) 'The careers officer: a marginalised member of the education family?', *School Organisation*, 12 (1): 99–111.

Martin, S. (1995) Choosing a Secondary School: Can Parents' Behaviour Be Described as Rational?, paper presented at British Educational Research Conference, Bath, 1995.

National Statistics (2005) *Statistical First Release* 03/2005. London: DfES.

National Statistics (2005) *Census 2001* [on-line]. London: ONS. Available from: http://www.statistics.gov.uk/census2001/census2001.asp

National Statistics (2006) *Education and Training* [on-line]. London: ONS. Available from: http://www.statistics.gov.uk/CCI/nscl.asp?ID=5005&x=11&y=4

Nice, R. (1997) 'Bourdieu and Bernstein'. Plenary Lecture, Pierre Bourdieu: Language, Culture and Education: An International Conference. Southampton University, 17–18 April, 1997.

ONS (2006) *Neighbourhood Statistics* [on-line]. London: ONS. Available from: http://neighbourhood.statistics.gov.uk/dissemination/

Osipow, S. H. (1990) 'Convergence in theories of career choice and development: review and prospect', *Journal of Vocational Behaviour*, 36: 122–131.

Paterson, L. and Raffe, D. (1995) 'Staying-on in full-time education in Scotland, 1985–1991', *Oxford Review of Education*, 21 (3): 3–23.

Payne, J. (1995) *Routes Beyond Compulsory Schooling*. DfES Research Report 31. London: DfES.

Payne, J. (1998) *Routes at 16: Trends and Choices in the Nineties*. DfES Research Report 55. London: DfES.

Payne, J. (2001a) *Work-based Training for Young People: Data from the England and Wales Youth Cohort Study*. DfES Research Report 276. London: DfES.

Payne, J. (2001b) *Patterns of Participation in Full-time Education after 16: An Analysis of the England and Wales Youth Cohort Study*. DfES Research Report 307. London: DfES.

Payne, J. (2003) *Choice at the end of compulsory schooling: A Research Review*. DfES Research Report 414. London: DfES.

Pitman, M. and Maxwell, J. (1992) 'Qualitative approaches to evaluation: models and methods', in M. LeCompte, W. Millroy, and J. Preissle (Eds), *The Handbook of Qualitative Research in Education*. San Diego: Academic Press.

QCA (2000) *Qualifications 16–19: A Guide to the Changes Resulting from the Qualifying for Success Consultation*. London: Qualifications and Curriculum Authority.

Raffe, D. and Willms, J. D. (1989) 'Schooling the discouraged worker: Local labour market effects on educational participation', *Sociology*, 23: 559-81.

Reay, D. (1995) ' "They employ cleaners to do that": habitus in the primary classroom', *British Journal of Sociology of Education*, 16 (3): 353–371.

Reay, D. (2002) 'Class, authenticity and the transition to higher education for mature students', *The Sociological Review*, 50 (3): 398–418.

Reay, D. and Ball, S. (1998) ' "Making their minds up": family dynamics of school choice', *British Educational Research Journal*, 24 (4): 431–448.

Reay, D., David, M. and Ball, S. J. (2001) 'Making a difference? Institutional habituses and higher education choice', *Sociological Research Online*, 5 (4): 126–142.

Reay, D. and Lucey, H. (2003) 'The limits of "Choice": Children and inner city schooling', *Sociology*, 37 (1): 121–142.

Rees, G., Fervre, R., Furlong, J. and Gorard, S. (1997) 'History, place and the learning society: Towards a sociology of lifetime learning', in *Journal of Education Policy*, 12 (6): 485–497.

Richards, C. (2005) 'Securing the self: Risk and aspiration in the post-16 curriculum', *British Journal of Sociology of Education*, 26 (5): 613–625.

Roberts, K. (1968) 'The entry into employment: an approach towards a general theory', *Sociological Review*, 16 (2): 165–184.

Roberts, K. (1975) 'The developmental theory of occupational choice: a critique and alternative', in G. Esland *et al.* (Eds), *People and Work*. Edinburgh: Holme McDougal.

Roberts, K. (1977) 'The social conditions, consequences and limitations of careers guidance', *British Journal of Guidance and Counselling*, 5: 1–9.

Roberts, K. (1995) *Youth and Employment in Modern Britain*. Oxford: Oxford University Press.

Roberts, K. (1997a) 'Structure and agency: the new youth research agenda', in J. Bynner, L. Chisholm and A. Furlong (Eds), *Youth, Citizenship and Social Change in a European Context*. Aldershot: Ashgate.

Roberts, K. (1997b) 'Prolonged transitions to uncertain destinations: the implications for careers guidance', *British Journal of Guidance and Counselling*, 25 (3): 345–360.

Rudd, P. (1997) 'From socialisation to postmodernity: a review of theoretical perspectives on the school-to-work transition', *Journal of Education and Work*, 10 (3): 257–279.

Rudd, P. and Evans, K. (1998) 'Structure and agency in youth transitions: student experiences of vocational further education', *Journal of Youth Studies*, 1 (1): 39–62.
Ryrie, A. (1981) *Routes and Results: A Study of the Later Years of Schooling*. London: Hodder & Stoughton/Scottish Council for Research in Education.
Seale, C. (1999) *The Quality of Quantitative Research*. London: Sage.
See, B. H., Gorard, S. and White, P. (2004) 'Teacher demand: crisis, what crisis?', *Cambridge Journal of Education*, 34 (1): 103–123.
Selwyn, N. (1999) 'Information technology and the A-level curriculum: a core skill or a fringe benefit?', *Research Papers in Education*, 14 (2): 123–137.
Silverman, D. (1985) *Qualitative Methodology and Sociology*. Aldershot: Gower.
Silverman, D. (1993) *Interpreting Qualitative Data: Methods for Analysing Talk, Text and Interaction*. London: Sage.
Silverman, D. (2000) *Doing Qualitative Research: A Practical Handbook*. London: Sage.
Sjöberg, L. (2005) 'The importance of respect for empirical findings', *Journal of Risk Research*, 8: 713–715.
Smedley, D. (1995) 'Marketing schools to parents – some lessons from the research on parental choice', *Educational Management and Administration*, 23 (2): 96–103.
Smith, E. (2003a) 'Failing boys and moral panics: perspectives on the underachievement debate', *British Journal of Educational Studies*, 51 (3): 282–295.
Smith, E. (2003b) 'Understanding underachievement: an investigation into the differential achievement of secondary school pupils', *British Journal of Sociology of Education*, 24 (5): 575–586.
Smith, E. (2005) *Analysing Underachievement in Schools*. London: Continuum.
Stager, D. (1996) 'Returns to investment in Ontario university education 1960–1990 and implications for tuition fee policy', *Canadian Journal of Higher Education*, 26 (2): 1–22.
Strauss, A. (1962) 'Transformations of identity', in A. M. Rose (Ed.), *Human Behaviour and Social Processes: An Interactionist Approach*. London: Routledge and Kegan Paul.
Sullivan, A. (2002a) 'Bourdieu and education: how useful is Bourdieu's theory for researchers?', *Netherlands' Journal of Social Sciences*, 38 (2): 144–166.
Sullivan, A. (2002b) 'Students as rational decision-makers: the question of beliefs and desires'. Mimeo. Nuffield College, Oxford.
Super, D. E. (1957) *The Psychology of Careers*. New York: Harper and Row.
Super, D. E. (1968) 'A theory of vocational development', in B. Hobson and J. Hayes (Eds), *The Theory and Practice of Vocational Guidance*. Oxford: Pergamon Press.
Super, D. E. (1981) 'Approaches to occupational choice and career development', in A. G. Watts, D. E. Super and J. M. Kidd (Eds), *Career Development in Britain*. Cambridge: Hobsons Press.
Taylor, M. J. (1992) 'Post-16 options: young people's awareness, attitudes, intentions and influences on their choice', *Research Papers in Education*, 7 (3): 301–335.

Thomas, W., Webber, D. and Walton, F. (2002) 'The school leaving intentions at the age of 16: evidence from a multicultural city environment', *Economic Issues* 7 (1), 1–14.

Van de Werfhorst, H., Sullivan, A. and Cheung, S. I. (2003) 'Social class, ability and choice of subject in secondary and tertiary education in Britain', *British Educational Research Journal*, 29 (1): 41–62.

Vincent, D. and Dean, J. (1977) *One Year Courses in Colleges and Sixth Forms*. Slough: NfER.

West, A., David, M., Hailes, J. and Ribbens, J. (1995) 'Parents and the process of choosing secondary schools: implications for schools', *Educational Management and Administration*, 23 (1): 28–38.

West, A. and Varlaam, A. (1991) 'Choosing a secondary school: parents of junior school children', *Educational Research*, 33 (1): 22–30.

White, P. (2002) Choices and Trajectories: Decision-Making in Compulsory Schooling and the Transition to Post-16 Education, Training and Work. Unpublished PhD thesis. Cardiff University: School of Social Sciences.

White, P., Gorard, S. and See, B. H. (2006) 'What are the problems with teacher supply?', *Teachers and Teacher Education*, 22 (3): 315–326.

Willis, P. (1977) *Learning to Labour*. Farnborough: Saxon House.

Young, S. (1994) 'Beware the Perils of Parental Power', *Times Educational Supplement*, 06/05/94, p. 2.

Index

achievement
  gaps, 61–3
  low, 89
agency, *see* structure
anecdotalism, 25, 33, 45
attainment, *see* achievement

Bourdieu, Pierre, 6, 27, 33, 168

capital, 6
  cultural, 5–6
  social, 6
  human, 6
careers
  education and guidance (CEG), 3, 22–3, 34, 146, 169
  teachers and advisors, **23–4**, 136
class, 19, 71–2, 57–60
  intermediate, 178
  knowledge, 29
  middle, 7, 28–30
  occupational, 13, 30–1, 40, 57–60
  and occupational aspirations, **158–9**
  operationalisation, 7
  service, 29–30, 161–5
  social, 7, 11, 12, 14, 28–33, 61
  working, 159–60
context
  historical, **47–82**, 155
continuity, 18, 135
convenience, **137–40**
cost, financial, 139
courses
  one-year, 50–1
  specialist, 143–5, 168
culture
  financial, 164
  institutional, 23
  pedagogical, 134
Curriculum 2000, 20

Diploma of Vocational Education (DOVE), 160

Economic and Social Research Council (ESRC), 12
ethnicity, 61, **175**

facilities, *see* resources
friends, 141–2
functionalism, 2
further education, **53–6**

gender, 20, 61, **156–8**, *see also* sex

habitus, 5–6, 26
happiness, 28
higher education, **56–60**, 74, 124–7
  Age Participation Index (API), 56–60, 66
  choice, 19
  and class, 19, 57–60
  Initial Entry Rate (IER), 56–7

industry
  manufacturing, 156
information
  sources, **20–4**
  formal *v.* informal, 21
institutions
  choice of, **79–80**
instrumental attitudes, 34

knowledge, folk, 117

longitudinal studies, 10, 13, 18

media studies, 131
mixed method studies, 13, 16

models
  of decision-making, **98–102**
Modern Apprenticeships, 89
multivariate analysis, 12, 18–19, 64, 167

non-response, 36

occupational, aspirations *v.* expectations, 10–13, 153–5
opportunity structure, 3

parents' education, 70–1
peers, *see* friends
percentages *v.* percentage points, 57–60
proximity, 18, 144
psychology, 75, 3
  developmental, 2, 3–4

qualifications
  choice of, **73–5**
  levels, 56
  parity of esteem, 150

rational action theory, 7–9, 28
rationality, 8, 24, 26–7, 28
rationalisation, *post hoc*, 41
'reflection effect', 135
reputation, 17, 20
  academic, 17
  local, 132–3
residential courses, 145
resources, specialist, 86, 136–7
rurality, 88

sample
  of educational institutions, **39**
  student, **39–40**
school
  choice, 8–9, 15, 18, 24–5
  effect, 24, 64–5, 169
  grammar, 161–3
  independent, 63–5
  types, 38, **63–5**, 69–70
Scottish School Leavers Survey (SSLS), 21, 60
security, 18, 110
sex, 18, 63, 77–8, *see also* gender
  and aspirations, **155–8**
  and course choice, 51–2
  and subject choice, 77
short-termism, 120
social
  background, 4–5, 18
  reproduction, **4–9**
socio-economic status (SES), 12, 18
staying-on, **16**, 17–18, 22–3, 64
structure
  and agency, 3–4, 33
  occupational, 48
structural factors, 5, 12
subjects
  choice of, **75–9**
  enjoyment of, 127–8
  new, 131
  differential attainment in, 78–9
  declining, 76
  growing, 75
  performance in, **110–12**
  utility of, **115–18**

timing
  of interviews, **41–2**
Tomlinson Report, 171
transport
  public, 137–8
travel, 18, **137–40**, 143–5

values, normative, 125

work experience, 162–4

Youth Cohort Study (YCS), 19, 22–3, 36–7, 53, 60, 73–5, 79, 167–8